John Smith

A description of New England

or observations and discoveries in the north of America in the year of Our

Lord 1614

John Smith

A description of New England
or observations and discoveries in the north of America in the year of Our Lord 1614

ISBN/EAN: 9783337645212

Printed in Europe, USA, Canada, Australia, Japan

Cover: Foto ©ninafisch / pixelio.de

More available books at **www.hansebooks.com**

A DESCRIPTION

OF

ℕew 𝔈ngland;

OR,

OBSERVATIONS AND DISCOVERIES
IN THE NORTH OF AMERICA
IN THE YEAR OF OUR LORD 1614.

With the Success of six Ships that went the next year, 1615.

BY CAPTAIN JOHN SMITH.

(Admiral of that Country.)

With a Fac-simile of the Original Map.

Boston:
WILLIAM VEAZIE.
M DCCC LXV.

PUBLISHER'S PREFACE.

HE "Description of New England," by Captain John Smith, is one of the most important works to be found relating to the history of this part of the country. It is the first book in which the country described by him, previously called *North Virginia*, is styled *New England*. The edition here given is an exact reprint — though not intended as a *fac-simile* — of the original tract, a copy of which the publisher had the privilege of using while the work was going through the press.

Smith's map of *New England* was first published in this tract. It was subsequently re-issued in other works of Smith ; additions being made on the engraved copper-plate, from time to time, to indicate the more recent discoveries and settlements. The map is thus found in *nine* different conditions, the latest having been issued four years after the death of Smith (which took place in 1631), in a work by another author.

The map as at first published was, of course, in its simplest form, and copies in this condition are now rarely to be met with. The only one known to Mr. Charles Deane, who, with Mr. James Lenox of New York, some years since, collated many copies of the map, is in the *Prince Library* of the *Old South Church*, in Boston. It is in a copy of the *Description of New England*, which contains, in Prince's autograph, the following : " *T. Prince, Sud-*

bury, in England, June 1, 1713." That this impression of the map was struck from the plate in its original condition is also shown by the fact that the transcript published by Hulsius the next year, in his translation of Smith's tract, corresponds to this, except that the names of the engraver and printer, in the lower corners, are omitted, and Smith's title, the verses below the portrait, and some of the explanations, are in German.

The reprint of the map here published is an exact *fac-simile* of Prince's copy, re-engraved on copper.

It is interesting to notice that many of the names which our towns and cities now bear are given on the map to prominent places on the coast; but *Plymouth* and *Cape Anna* are the only places which have retained them. Smith gave the name *Charles River* to the water that he saw coming out of Boston harbor, which he never entered; but that name was subsequently transferred to one of the streams running into this harbor.

This tract was reprinted, with some variations, in Smith's larger work, the *Generall Historie*, first published in 1624. This latter work also embraced the most of Smith's tracts issued up to that time. The *Description* has been reprinted by the Massachusetts Historical Society, in vol. vi., third series, of their Collections, 1837; and is also included in the second volume of Force's tracts, 1838.

It is quite unnecessary to enter here into a detailed account of Captain Smith's career, as his biography is easily accessible to all, and we have nothing new to add to it. After leaving *Virginia* (where he had spent about two years and a half) in the autumn of 1609, we lose sight of him till 1614. On the 3d of March of that year, he left the Downs with two vessels, fitted out at the joint charge of four London merchants and himself, for *New England*, where he arrived the last of April. He was absent on this voyage about six months. His adventures and discoveries here are best told by himself in the ensuing narrative. It will be seen that he made two unsuccessful attempts to reach these shores the next year. In consideration of his labors in the cause of *New-England* colonization, and of the interest he continued to feel in this object, the Plymouth Company conferred upon him the title of *Admiral of New England.* It was doubtless expected that he would soon return to the country, which he desired to do ; but he met with many obstacles, and never again visited *New England.* Nothing appears to have been directly effected by his agency in the way of permanent colonization here ; though he continued to favor emigration, and distributed thousands of his books and maps, which doubtless stimulated the pursuit of fishing upon the coast, by which a better knowledge of the country may have been gained, and spread abroad. The settlement of *Plymouth* in 1620 — the first permanent colony in New England—was, as is well known, accidental. The destination of the *Mayflower* was not the shores of New England, although the Pilgrims were familiar with Smith's map of our coast.

We give below, in an abridged form, the titles of Smith's different works ; viz. : —

A True Relation, &c. London, 1608.
A Map of Virginia, &c. Oxford, 1612.
A Description of New England, &c. London, 1616.
New Englands Trials, &c. London, 1620. Second ed., 1622.
The Generall Historie, &c. London, 1624. Also re-issued (not reprinted) in 1626, 1627, and twice in 1632, the year after Smith's death ; the date on the titlepage being altered to correspond to those years.
An Accidence, or the Pathway to Experience, &c. London, 1626.
A Sea Grammar, &c. London, 1627. Other editions, 1653 and 1692.
The True Travels, &c. London, 1630.
Advertisements for the Unexperienced Planters of New-England, &c. London, 1631.

The Publisher would express his acknowledgments to Mr. Deane for the bibliographical and historical information contained in this prefatory note.

Boston, May 1, 1865.

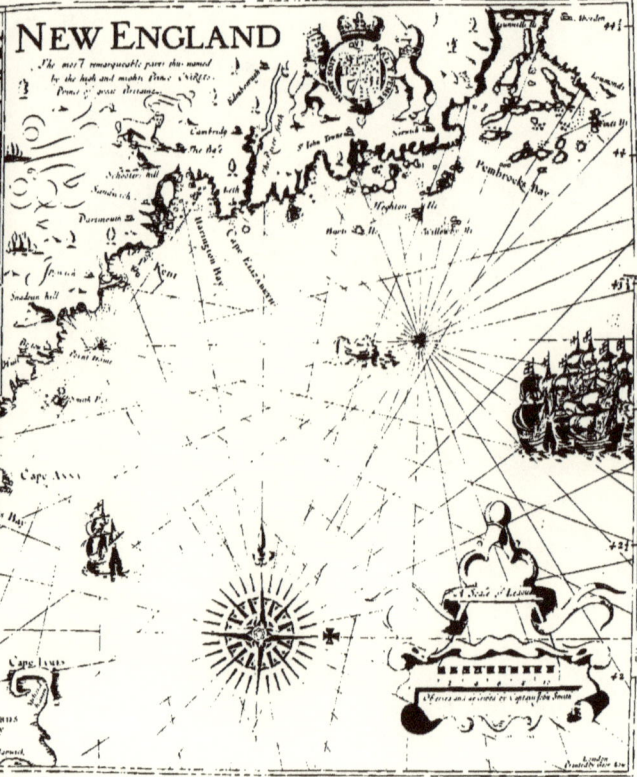

A

DESCRIPTION

of New-England:

O R

THE OBSERVATIONS, AND

Difcoueries of Captain *Iohn. Smith* (Admirall
of that Country) in the North of *America*, in the year
of our Lord 1614: *with the fucceffe of fixe Ships,
that went the next yeare* 1615 ; *and the*
accidents befell him among the
French men of warre:

With the proofe of the prefent benefit this
Countrey affoords: whither this prefent yeare,
1616, *eight voluntary Ships are gone
to make further tryall.*

At LONDON

Printed by *Humfrey Lownes,* for *Robert Clerke ;* and
are to be fould at his houfe called the Lodge,
in Chancery lane, ouer againft Lin-
colnes Inne. 1616.

TO THE HIGH
HOPEFVL Charles,

Prince of Great Britaine.

SIR:

O fauourable was your moſt renowned and memorable Brother, Prince *Henry*, to all generous deſignes; that in my diſcouery of *Virginia*, I preſumed to call two nameleſſe Headlands after my Soueraignes heires, *Cape Henry* and *Cape Charles*. Since then, it beeing my chance to range ſome other parts of *America*, whereof I heere preſent your Highneſs the deſcription in a Map; my humble ſute is, you would pleaſe to change their Barbarous names, for ſuch *Engliſh*, as Poſterity may ſay, Prince *Charles* was their Godfather. What here in this relation I promiſe my Countrey, let mee liue or die the ſlaue of ſcorne and infamy, if (hauing meanes) I make it not apparent; pleaſe God to bleſſe me but from ſuch accidents as are beyond my power and reaſon to preuent. For my labours, I deſire but ſuch conditions as were promiſed me out of the gaines; and that your Highneſſe would daigne to grace this Work, by your Princely and fauourable reſpect vnto it, and know mee to be

Your Highneſſ true
and faithful ſeruant,

Iohn Smith.

TO THE RIGHT HONOUR-
able and worthy Lords, Knights,
and Gentlemen, of his Ma-
iefties Councell, for all Planta-
tions and difcoueries ; efpecially,
of New England.

Eeing the deedes of the moſt iuſt, and the writings of the moſt wiſe, not onely of men, but of God himſelfe, haue beene diuerſly traduced by variable iudgments of the Times opinioniſts ; what ſhall ſuch an ignorant as I expect ? Yet repoſing myſelfe on your fauours, I preſent this rude difcourſe, to the worldes conſtruction ; though I am perſwaded, that few do think there may be had from *New England* Staple commodities, well worth 3 or 400000 pound a yeare, with ſo ſmall charge, and ſuch facilitie, as this difcourſe will acquaint you. But, leſt your Honours, that know mee not, ſhould thinke I goe by hearefay or affections ; I intreat your pardons to ſay thus much of myſelfe : Neere twice nine yeares, I haue beene taught by lamentable experience, as well in *Europe* and *Aſia*, as *Affrick* and *America*, ſuch honeſt aduentures as the chance of warre doth caſt vpon poor ſouldiers. So that, if I bee not able

to

to iudge of what I haue feene, contriued, and done; it is not the fault either of my eyes, or foure quarters. And thefe nine yeares, I haue bent my endeauours to finde a fure foundation to begin thefe enfuing proiects: which though I neuer fo plainely and ferioufly propound; yet it refteth in God, and you, ftill to difpofe of. Not doubting but your goodneffe will pardon my rudeneffe, and ponder errours in the balance of good will; No more: but facring all my beft abilities to the good of my Prince, and Countrey, and fubmitting my felfe to the exquifit iudgements of your renowned vertue, I euer reft

Your Honours, in

all honeft feruice,

I. S.

To the right Worſhipfull Aduenturers
for the Countrey of NewEngland, in the
Cities of *London, Briſtow, Exceter, Plymouth,*
Dartmouth, Baſtable, Totneys, &c.
and in all other Cities and Ports,
in the Kingdome
of *England.*

F the little Ant, and the ſillie Bee ſeek by their diligence the good of their Commonwealth ; much more ought Man. If they puniſh the drones and ſting them ſteales their labour; then blame not Man. Little hony hath that hiue, where there are more Drones then Bees : and miſerable is that Land, where more are idle then well imployed. If the indeauours of thoſe vermin be acceptable, I hope mine may be excuſeable ; Though I confeſſe it were more proper for mee, To be doing what I ſay, then writing what I knowe. Had I returned rich, I could not haue erred : Now hauing onely ſuch fiſh as came to my net, I muſt be taxed. But, I would my taxers were as ready to adventure their purſes, as I, purſe, life, and all I haue : or as diligent to furniſh the charge, as I know they are vigilant to crop the fruits of my labours. Then would I not doubt (did God pleaſe I might ſafely arriue in *New England,* and ſafely returne) but to performe ſomewhat more then I haue promiſed, and approue my words by deeds, according to proportion.

I am not the firſt hath beene betrayed by Pirats : And foure

men

men of warre, prouided as they were, had beene fufficient to haue taken *Sampfon*, *Hercules*, and *Alexander* the great, no other way furnifht then I was. I knowe not what affurance any haue do paffe the Seas, Not to be fubiect to cafualty as well as my felfe : but leaft this difafter may hinder my proceedings, or ill will (by rumour) the behoofefull worke I pretend ; I haue writ this little : which I did think to haue concealed from any publike vfe, till I had made my returnes fpeake as much, as my pen now doth.

But becaufe I fpeak fo much of fifhing, if any take mee for fuch a deuote fifher, as I dreame of nought elfe, they miftake mee. I know a ring of golde from a graine of barley, as well as a goldefmith : and nothing is there to bee had which fifhing doth hinder, but furder vs to obtaine. Now for that I haue made knowne vnto you a fit place for plantation, limited within the bounds of your Patent and Commiffion ; hauing alfo recciued meanes, power, and authority by your directions to plant there a Colony, and make further fearch and difcouery in thofe parts there yet vnknowne : Confidering, withall, firft thofe of his Maiefties Councell, then thofe Cities aboue named, and diuerfe others that haue beene moued to lend their affiftance to fo great a work, do expect (efpecially the aduenturers) the true relation or euent of my proceedings which I heare are fo abufed ; I am inforced for all thefe refpects, rather to expofe my imbecillitie to contempt, by the teftimonie of thefe rude lines then all fhould condemne me for fo bad a Factor, as could neither giue reafon nor account of my actions and defignes.

Yours to command,

Iohn Smith.

In the deserued Honour of the Author,
Captaine Iohn Smith, and his Worke.

*D*Amn'd Enuie is a fp'rite, that euer haunts
   Beafts, mif-nam'd men ; Cowards, or Ignorants.
But, onely fuch fhee followes, whofe deere WORTH
(Maugre her malice) fets their glorie forth.
  If this faire Ouerture, then, take not ; It
  Is Enuie's *fpight (dear friend) in men-of-wit ;*
Or Feare, *left morfels, which our mouthes poffeffe,*
Might fall from thence ; or elfe, tis Scottifhneffe.
  If either ; (I hope neither,) thee they raife ;
  Thy* Letters are as Letters in thy praife ;
Who, by their vice, improue *(when they* reprooue)
Thy vertue ; fo, in hate, procure thee Loue.
  Then, On firme Worth : this Monument I frame ;
  Scorning for any Smith to forge *fuch* fame.

* *Hinderers.*   Io : Dauies, *Heref :*

To his worthy Captaine the Author.

*T*Hat which wee call the fubiect of all Storie,
   Is Truth : which in this Worke of thine giues glorie
To all that thou haft done. Then, fcorne the fpight
Of Enuie ; which doth no mans merits right.
  My fword may help the reft : my pen no more
  Can doe, but this ; I'aue faid enough before.
          Your fometime fouldier,
             I. Codrinton, *now Templer.*

2

To my Worthy friend and Coufen,
Captaine Iohn Smith.

IT ouer-ioyes my heart, when as thy Words
  Of thefe defignes, with deeds I doe compare.
Heere is a Booke, fuch worthy truth affords,
None fhould the due defert thereof impare ;
Sith thou, the man, deferuing of thefe Ages,
Much paine haft ta'en for this our Kingdoms good,
In *Climes vnknowne, Mongft* Turks *and Saluages,*
T'inlarge our bounds ; though with thy loffe of blood.
  Hence damn'd Detraction : ftand not in our way,
  Enuie, it felfe, will not the Truth gainefay.

N. Smith.

To that worthy and generous Gentle-
man, my verie good friend, *Captaine Smith.*

MAy Fate thy Profpect profper, that thy name
   May be eternifed with liuing fame :
Though foule Detraction Honour would peruert,
And Ennie euer waits vpon defert :
In fpight of Pelias, when his hate lies colde,
Returne as Iafon with a fleece of Golde.
  Then after-ages fhall record thy praife,
  That a New England to this Ile didft raife :
And when thou dyft (as all that liue muft die)
Thy fame liue heere ; thou, with Eternitie.

R: Gunnell.

To his friend Cap: Smith vpon his
defcription of New England.

*S*Ir; your Relations I haue read: which fhewe
    Their's reafon I fhould honour them and you ;
And if their meaning I haue vnderflood,
I dare to cenfure, thus : Your Proiect's good ;
And may (if follow'd) doubtleffe quit the paine,
With honour, pleafure and a treeble gaine ;
Befide the benefit that fhall arife
To make more happie our Poftcritics.

    For would we daigne to fpare, though 'twere no more
Then what o're-filles, and furfets vs in ftore,
To order Nature's fruitfulneffe a while
In that rude Garden, you New England ftile ;
With prefent good, ther's hope in after-daies
Thence to repaire what Time and Pride decaies
In this rich kingdome. And the fpatious Weft
Being ftill more with Englifh blood poffeft,
The Proud Iberians fhall not rule thofe Seas,
To checke our fhips from fayling where they pleafe ;
Nor future times make any forraine power
Become fo great to force a bound to Our.

    Much good my minde fore-tels would follow hence
With little labour, and with leffe expence.
Thriue therefore thy Defigne, who ere enuie :
England may ioy in England's Colony,
Virginia feeke her Virgine fifters good,
Be bleffed in fuch happie neighbourhood :
    Or, what-foere Fate pleafeth to permit,
    Be thou ftill honor'd for firft mooning it.

George Wither,
è focietate Lincols.

In the deſerued honour of my honeſt
and worthie Captaine, Iohn Smith,
and his Worke.

*C*Aptaine *and friends when I peruſe thy booke*
  (With Iudgements *eyes) into thy* heart *I looke:*
*And there I finde (what ſometimes-*Albyon *knew)*
A Souldier, *to his* Countries-honour, *true.*
  Some fight for wealth ; *and ſome for* emptie praiſe ;
  But thou alone thy Countries Fame *to raiſe.*
With due diſcretion, *and* vndanted heart,
I (oft) ſo well haue ſeene thee act thy Part
  In deepeſt plunge of hard extreamitie,
  As forc't the troups of proudeſt foes to flie.
Though men of greater Ranke *and leſſe* deſert
Would Piſh-*away thy* Praiſe, *it can not ſtart*
  From the true Owner ; *for, all good-mens tongues*
  Shall keepe the ſame.   To them that Part belongs.
If, then, Wit, Courage, *and* Succeſſe *ſhould get*
Thee Fame ; *the Muſe for* that *is in thy* debt :
  A part whereof (leaſt able though I bee)
  Thus heere I doe diſburſe, to honor Thee.

Rawly Croshaw.

Michael Phettiplace, William Phettiplace, &

Richard Wiffing, *Gentlemen, and*
Souldiers vnder Captaine *Smiths*
Command: In his deserued
honor for his Worke,
and worth.

WHy may not we in this Worke haue our Mite,
   That had our share in each black day and night,
When thou Virginia *soild'st, yet kept'st vnstained;*
And held'st the King of Paspeheh *enchained.*
Thou all alone in Saluage *sterne didst take.*

  Pamunkes *king wee saw thee captiue make*
Among seauen hundred of his stoutest men,
To murther thee and vs resolued; when
Fast by the hand thou ledst this Saluage grim,
Thy Pistoll at his breast to gouerne him:
Which did infuse such awe in all the rest
(Sith their drad Soueraigne thou had'st so distrest)
That thou and wee (poore sixteene) safe retir'd
Vnto our helplesse ships.   *Thou (thus admir'd)*
Didst make proud Powhatan, *his subiects send*
To Iames *his Towne, thy censure to attend:*
And all Virginia's *Lords, and Pettie Kings,*
Aw'd by thy vertue, crouch, and Presents brings
To gaine thy grace; so dreaded thou hast beene:
And yet a heart more milde is seldome seene;
So, making Valour Vertue, really;
Who hast nought in thee counterfet, or slie:
If in the sleight bee not the truest art,
That makes men famoused for faire desert.

                           Who

Who faith of thee, this fauors of vaine-glorie,
Miftakes both thee and vs, and this true ftorie.
If it bee ill in Thee, fo well to doe;
Then, is it ill in Vs, to praife thee too,
But, if the firft bee well done; it is well,
To fay it doth (if fo it doth) excel!
Praife is the guerdon of each deere defert,
Making the praifed act the praifed part
With more alacritie: Honours *Square is* Praife;
Without which, it (regardleffe) foone decaies.

And for this paines of thine wee praife thee rather,
That future times may know who was the father
Of this rare *Worke* (New England) *which may bring
Praife to thy God, and profit to thy King.*

Because the Booke was printed ere

the Prince his Highneffe had altered the names, I intreate
the Reader, perufe this fchedule ; which will
plainely fhew him the correfpondence
of the old names to the new.

The old names.	The new.	The old names.	The new.
Cape Cod	Cape Iames	Sowocatuck	Ipfwitch
	Milford hauen	Bahana	Dartmouth
Chawum	Barwick		Sandwich
Accomack	Plimouth	Aucocifcos Mount	Shooters hill
Sagoquas	Oxford	Aucocifco	The Bafe
Maffachufets Mount	Cheuit hill	Aumoughcawgen	Cambridge
Maffachufets Riuer	Charles Riuer	Kinebeck	Edenborough
Totant	Fawmouth	Sagadahock	Leeth
A Country not difcouerd	Briftow	Pemmaquid	S. Iohns towne
Naemkeck	Baftable	Monahigan	Barties Iles
Cape Trabigzanda	Cape Anne	Segocket	Norwich
Aggawom	Southampton	Matinnack	Willowby's Iles
Smiths Iles	Smiths Iles	Metinnicus	Hoghton's Iles
Paffataquack	Hull	Mecadacut	Dunbarton
Accominticus	Bofton	Pennobfcot	Aborden
Saffanowes Mount	Snodon hill	Nufket	Lowmonds

A DESCRIPTION OF
New-England, by Captaine
Iohn Smith.

I N the moneth of Aprill, 1614. with *My first voyage to New-England* two Ships from *London*, of a few Marchants, I chanced to ariue in *New-England*, a parte of *Amcryca*, at the Ile of *Mona-higgan*, in 43½ of Northerly latitude: our plot was there to take Whales and make tryalls of a Myne of Gold and Copper. If thofe failed, Fifh and Furres was then our refuge, to make our felues fauers howfoeuer: we found this Whalefifhing a coftly conclufion: we faw many, and fpent much time in chafing them; but could not kill any: They beeing a kinde of Iubartes, and not the Whale that yeeldes Finnes and Oyle as wee expected. For our Golde, it was rather the Mafters deuice to get a voyage that pro-iected it, then any knowledge hee had at all of any fuch matter. Fifh and Furres was now our guard: and by our late arriual, and long lingring about the Whale, the prime of both thofe feafons were paft ere wee perceiued it;

we

we thinking that their feafons ferued at all times: but wee
found it otherwife; for by the midft of Iune, the fifhing
failed.   Yet in Iuly and Auguft fome was taken, but not
fufficient to defray fo great a charge as our ftay required.
Of dry fifh we made about 40000. of Cor fifh about 7000.
Whileft the failers fifhed, my felfe with eight or nine others
of them might beft bee fpared; Ranging the coaft in a fmall
boat, wee got for trifles neer 1100 Beuer fkinnes, 100 Martins, and neer as many Otters; and the moft of them within
the diftance of twenty leagues.   We ranged the Coaft both
Eaft and Weft much furder; but Eaftwards our commodities were not efteemed, they were fo neare the French who
affords them better: and right againft vs in the Main was a
Ship of Sir *Frances Popphames*, that had there fuch acquaintance, hauing many yeares vfed onely that porte, that the
moft parte there was had by him.   And 40 leagues weft-
wards were two French Ships, that had made there a great
voyage by trade, during the time wee tryed thofe conclufions, not knowing the Coaft, nor Saluages habitation.
With thefe Furres, the Traine, and Cor-fifh I returned for
England in the Bark: where within fix monthes after our
departure from the *Downes*, we fafe arriued back.   The
beft of this fifh was folde for fiue pound the hundreth, the
reft by ill vfage betwixt three pound and fifty fhillings.
The other Ship ftaied to fit herfelfe for *Spaine* with the dry
fifh which was fould, by the Sailers reporte that returned,

at

at forty ryalls the quintall, each hundred weighing two
quintalls and a halfe.

New England is that part of *America* in the   *The situation of*
Ocean Sea oppofite to *Noua Albyon* in the South   *New England.*
Sea; difcouered by the moft memorable Sir *Francis Drake*
in his voyage about the worlde.   In regarde whereto this
is ftiled *New England*, beeing in the fame latitude.   *New
France*, off it, is Northward: Southwardes is *Virginia*, and
all the adioyning Continent, with *New Granado, New Spain,
New Andolofia* and the *Weft Indies*.   Now becaufe I haue
been fo oft afked fuch ftrange queftions, of the goodneffe
and greatneffe of thofe fpatious Tracts of land, how they
can bee thus long vnknown, or not poffeffed by the *Spaniard*, and many fuch like demands ;   I intreat your pardons,
if I chance to be too plaine, or tedious in relating my
knowledge for plaine mens fatiffaction.

Florida is the next adioyning to the *Indies*,
which vnprofperoufly was attempted to bee   *Notes of Florida.*
planted by the *French*.   A Country farre bigger then *England, Scotland, France* and *Ireland*, yet little knowne to any
Chriftian, but by the wonderful endeuours of *Ferdinando de
Soto* a valiant *Spaniard:* whofe writings in this age is the
beft guide knowne to fearch thofe parts.

Virginia is no Ile (as many doe imagine) but   *Notes of Vir-*
part of the Continent adioyning to *Florida;*   *ginia.*
whofe bounds may be ftreched to the magnitude thereof
without offence to any Chriftian inhabitant.   For from the
degrees

degrees of 30. to 45. his Maieftie hath granted his Letters
patents, the Coaft extending South-weft and North-eaft
aboute 1500 miles; but to follow it aboard, the fhore may
well be 2000. at the leaft: of which, 20. miles is the moft
giues entrance into the Bay of *Chifapeak*, where is the *London* plantation: within which is a Country (as you may
perceiue by the defcription in a Booke and Map printed in
my name of that little I there difcouered) may well fuffice
300000 people to inhabit. And Southward adioyneth that
part difcouered at the charge of Sir *Walter Rawley*, by Sir
Ralph Lane, and that learned Mathematician Mr. *Thomas
Heryot*. Northward fix or feauen degrees is the Riuer
Sagadahock, where was planted the Wefterne Colony, by
that Honourable Patrone of vertue Sir *Iohn Poppham*
Lord chief Iuftice of *England*. Ther is alfo a relation
printed by Captaine *Bartholomew Gofnould*, of *Elizabeths
Iles*: and an other by Captaine *Waymoth*, of *Pemmaquid*.
From all thefe diligent obferuers, pofterity may be bet-
tered by the fruits of their labours. But for diuers others
that long before and fince haue ranged thofe parts, within
a kenning fometimes of the fhore, fome touching in one
place fome in another, I muft entreat them pardon me for
omitting them; or if I offend in faying that their true
defcriptions are concealed, or neuer well obferued, or died
with the Authors: fo that the Coaft is yet ftill but euen as
a Coaft vnknowne and vndifcouered. I haue had fix or
feauen feuerall plots of thofe Northren parts, fo vnlike each

to

to other, and moft fo differing from any true proportion, or
refemblance of the Countrey, as they did mee no more
good, then fo much wafte paper, though they coft me more.
It may be it was not my chance to fee the beft; but leaft
others may be deceiued as I was, or through dangerous
ignorance hazard themfelues as I did, I haue drawen a
Map from Point to Point, Ile to Ile, and Harbour to Harbour, with the Soundings, Sands, Rocks, and Land-marks
as I paffed clofe aboard the Shore in a little Boat; although
there be many things to bee obferued which the hafte of
other affaires did caufe me omit: for, being fent more to
get prefent commodities, then knowledge by difcoueries for
any future good, I had not power to fearch as I would: yet
it will ferue to direct any fhall goe that waies, to fafe Harbours and the Saluages habitations: What marchandize
and commodities for their labour they may finde, this following difcourfe fhall plainely demonftrate.

Thus you may fee, of this 2000. miles more then halfe is
yet vnknowne to any purpofe: no not fo much as the borders of the Sea are yet certainly difcouered. As for the
goodnes and true fubftances of the Land, wee are for moft
part yet altogether ignorant of them, vnleffe it bee thofe
parts about the Bay of *Chifapeack* and *Sagadahock:* but
onely here and there wee touched or haue feene a little the
edges of thofe large dominions, which doe ftretch themfelues into the Maine, God doth know how many thoufand
miles; whereof we can yet no more iudge, then a ftranger
that

that faileth betwixt *England* and *France* can defcribe the
Harbors and dangers by landing here or there in fome
Riuer or Bay, tell thereby the goodneffe and fubftances of
Spaine, Italy, Germany, Bohemia, Hungaria and the reft.
By this you may perceiue how much they erre, that think
euery one which hath bin at *Virginia* vnderftandeth or
knowes what *Virginia* is : Or that the *Spaniards* know one
halfe quarter of thofe Territories they poffeffe ; no, not fo
much as the true circumference of *Terra Incognita*, whofe
large dominions may equalize the greatneffe and goodnes
of *America*, for any thing yet known.   It is ftrange with
what fmall power hee hath raigned in the *Eaſt Indies ;* and
few will vnderftand the truth of his ftrength in *America :*
where he hauing fo much to keepe with fuch a pampered
force, they neede not greatly feare his furie, in the *Bermu-
das, Virginia, New France*, or *New England ;* beyond whofe
bounds *America* doth ftretch many thoufand miles : into
the frozen partes whereof one Master *Hutfon* an Englifh
Mariner did make the greateft difcouerie of any Chriftian I
knowe of, where he vnfortunately died.   For *Affrica*, had
not the induftrious Portugales ranged her vnknowne parts,
who would haue fought for wealth among thofe fryed
Regions of blacke brutifh Negers, where notwithftanding
all the wealth and admirable aduentures and endeauours
more then 140 yeares, they knowe not one third of thofe
blacke habitations.   But it is not a worke for euery one, to
manage fuch an affaire as makes a difcouerie, and plants a
                                                    Colony :

Colony: It requires all the beſt parts of Art, Iudgement, Courage, Honeſty, Conſtancy, Dilligence and Induſtrie, to doe but neere well. Some are more proper for one thing then another; and therein are to be imployed: and nothing breedes more confuſion then miſplacing and miſimploying men in their vndertakings. *Columbus, Cortez, Pitzara, Soto, Magellanes,* and the reſt ſerued more then a prentiſhip to learne how to begin their moſt memorable attempts in the *Weſt Indes:* which to the wonder of all ages ſucceſfully they effected, when many hundreds of others farre aboue them in the worlds opinion, beeing inſtructed but by relation, came to ſhame and confuſion in actions of ſmall moment, who doubtleſſe in other matters, were both wiſe, diſcreet, generous, and couragious. I ſay not this to detract any thing from their incomparable merits, but to anſwer thoſe queſtionleſſe queſtions that keep vs back from imitating the worthineſſe of their braue ſpirits that aduanced themſelues from poore Souldiers to great Captaines, their poſterity to great Lords, their King to be one of the greateſt Potentates on earth, and the fruites of their labours, his greateſt glory, power and renowne.

That part wee call *New England* is betwixt the
degrees of 41. and 45: but that parte this diſcourſe
ſpeaketh of, ſtretcheth but from *Pennobſcot* to *Cape Cod,*
some 75 leagues by a right line diſtant each from other:
within which bounds I haue ſeene at leaſt 40. ſeuerall habitations vpon the Sea Coaſt, and founded about 25 excellent

The deſcription of New England.

good

good Harbours; In many whereof there is ancorage for
500. fayle of fhips of any burthen; in fome of them for
5000: And more than 200 Iles ouergrowne with good timber, of diuers forts of wood, which doe make fo many
harbours as requireth a longer time then I had, to be well
difcouered.

The particular Countries or Gou-ernments.   The principall habitation Northward we were
at, was *Pennobfcot:* Southward along the Coaft
and vp the Riuers we found *Mecadacut, Segocket,
Pemmaquid, Nufconcus, Kenebeck, Sagadahock,* and *Au-
moughcawgen;* And to thofe Countries belong the people
of *Segotago, Paghhuntanuck, Pocopaffum, Taughtanakag-
net, Warbigganus, Naffaque, Mafherofqueck, Wawrigweck,
Mofhoquen, Wakcogo, Pafharanack,* &c. To thefe are al-
lied the Countries of *Aucocifco, Accominticus, Paffataquack,
Aggawom,* and *Naemkeck:* all thefe, I could perceiue, differ
little in language, fafhion, or gouernment: though moft be
Lords of themfelues, yet they hold the *Bafhabes* of *Pennobfcot,* the chiefe and greateft amongft them.

The next I can remember by name are *Mattahunts;* two
pleafant Iles of groues, gardens and corne fields a league
in the Sea from the Mayne. Then *Totant, Maffachufet,
Pocapawmet, Quonahaffit, Sagoquas, Nahapaffumkeck, To-
peent, Seccafaw, Totheet, Nafnocomacak, Accomack, Chawum;* Then *Cape Cod* by which is *Pawmet and* the Ile
Nawfet of the language, and alliance of them of *Chawum:*
The others are called *Maffachufets;* of another language,
                                                     humor

humor and condition: For their trade and marchandize;
to each of their habitations they haue diuerfe Townes and
people belonging; and by their relations and defcriptions,
more then 20 feuerall Habitations and Riuers that ftretch
themfelues farre vp into the Countrey, euen to the borders
of diuerfe great Lakes, where they kill and take moft of
their Beuers and Otters. From *Pennobfcot* to *Sagadahock*
this Coaft is all Mountainous and Iles of huge Rocks, but
ouergrowen with all forts of excellent good woodes for
building houfes, boats, barks or fhippes; with an incredible
abundance of moft forts of fifh, much fowle, and fundry
forts of good fruites for mans vfe.

Betwixt *Sagadahock* and *Sowocatuck* there is *The mixture of*
but two or three fandy Bayes, but betwixt that *an excellent foyle.*
and *Cape Cod* very many: efpecialy the Coaft of the *Maf-*
fachufets is fo indifferently mixed with high clayie or fandy
cliffes in one place, and then tracts of large long ledges
of diuers forts, and quarries of ftones in other places fo
ftrangely diuided with trinctured veines of diuers colours:
as, Free ftone for building, Slate for tiling, fmooth ftone to
make Fornaces and Forges for glaffe or iron, and iron ore
fufficient, conueniently to melt in them: but the moft part
fo refembleth the Coaft of *Deuonfhire*, I thinke moft of the
cliffes would make fuch limeftone: If they be not of thefe
qualities, they are fo like, they may deceiue a better iudgement then mine; all which are fo neere adioyning to thofe
other aduantages I obferued in thefe parts, that if the Ore

4   proue

proue as good iron and fteele in thofe parts, as I know it is
within the bounds of the Countrey, I dare engage my head
(hauing but men fkilfull to worke the fimples there growing) to haue all things belonging to the building the rig-
ging of fhippes of any proportion, and good marchandize
for the fraught, within a fquare of 10 or 14 leagues: and
were it for a good rewarde, I would not feare to procure it
in a leffe limitation.

A proofe of an   .And furely by reafon of thofe fandy cliffes
excellent temper. and cliffes of rocks,˙ both which we faw fo
planted with Gardens and Corne fields, and fo well inhabited with a goodly, ftrong and well proportioned people,
A proofe of   befides the greatneffe of the Timber growing on
health.   them, the greatneffe of the fifh and moderate
temper of the ayre (for of twentie fiue, not any was ficke,
but two that were many yeares difeafed before they went
notwithftanding our bad lodging and accidentall diet) who
can but approoue this a moft excellent place, both for
health and fertility? And of all the foure parts of the
world that I haue yet feene not inhabited, could I haue but
meanes to tranfport a Colonie, I would rather liue here
then any where: and if it did not maintaine it felfe, were
wee but once indifferently well fitted, let vs ftarue.

Staple commodi-   The maine Staple, from hence to bee ex-
ties prefent.   tracted for the prefent to produce the reft, is
fifh; which howeuer it may feeme a mean and a bafe commoditie: yet who will but truely take the pains and confider

fider the fequell, I thinke will allow it well worth the labour. It is ftrange to fee what great aduentures the hopes of fetting forth men of war to rob the induftrious innocent, would procure; or fuch maffie promifes in groffe: though more are choked then well fedde with fuch haftie hopes. But who doth not know that the poore *The Hollanders* Hollanders, chiefly by fifhing, at a great charge *fifhing.* and labour in all weathers in the open Sea, are made a people fo hardy, and induftrious? and by the venting this poore commodity to the Eafterlings for as meane, which is Wood, Flax, Pitch, Tarre, Rofin, Cordage, and fuch like (which they exchange againe, to the French, Spaniards, Portugales, and Englifh, &c. for what they want) are made fo mighty, ftrong and rich, as no State but *Venice*, of twice their magnitude, is fo well furnifhed with fo many faire Cities, goodly Townes, ftrong Fortreffes, and that aboundance of fhipping and all forts of marchandize, as well of Golde, Siluer, Pearles, Diamonds, Pretious ftones, Silkes, Veluets, and Cloth of golde; as Fifh, Pitch, Wood, or fuch groffe commodities? What Voyages and Difcoueries, Eaft and Weft, North and South, yea about the world, make they? What an Army by Sea and Land, haue they long maintained in defpite of one of the greateft Princes of the world? And neuer could the Spaniard with all his Mynes of golde and Siluer, pay his debts, his friends, and army, halfe fo truly, as the Hollanders ftil haue done by this contemptible trade of fifh. Diuers (I know) may alledge, many

other

other affiftances : But this is their Myne ; and the Sea the fource of thofe filuered ftreames of all their vertue ; which hath made them now the very miracle of induftrie, the pattern of perfection for thefe affaires : and the benefit of fifhing is that *Primum mobile* that turnes all their *Spheres* to this height of plentie, ftrength, honour and admiration.

Herring, Cod, and Ling, is that triplicitie that makes their wealth and fhippings multiplicities, fuch as it is, and from which (few would thinke it) they yearly draw at leaft *Which is fifteen* one million and a halfe of pounds ftarling ; yet *hundred thou-* it is moft certaine (if records be true :) and in *fand pound.* this faculty they are fo naturalized, and of their vents fo certainly acquainted, as there is no likelihood they will euer bee paralleld, hauing 2 or 3000 Buffes, Flat bottomes, Sword pinks, Todes, and fuch like, that breedes them Saylers, Mariners, Souldiers and Marchants, neuer to be wrought out of that trade, and fit for any other. I will not deny but others may gaine as well as they, that will vfe it, though not fo certainely, nor fo much in quantity ; for want of experience. And this Herring they take vpon the Coaft of *Scotland* and *England ;* their Cod and Ling, vpon the Coaft of *Izeland* and in the North Seas.

Hamborough, and the *Eaft Countries,* for Sturgion and Cauiare, gets many thoufands of pounds from *England,* and the *Straites : Portugale,* the *Bifkaines,* and the *Spaniards,* make 40 or 50 Saile yearely to *Cape-blank,* to hooke for Porgos, Mullet, and make *Puttardo :* and *New found Land,*

Land, doth yearely fraught neere 800 fayle of Ships with a fillie leane fkinny Poore-Iohn, and Corfifh, which at leaft yearely amounts to 3 or 400000 pound. If from all thofe parts fuch paines is taken for this poore gaines of fifh, and by them hath neither meate, drinke, nor clothes, wood, iron, nor fteele, pitch, tarre, nets, leades, falt, hookes, nor lines, for fhipping, fifhing, nor prouifion, but at the fecond, third, fourth, or fifth hand, drawne from fo many feuerall parts of the world ere they come together to be vfed in this voyage: If thefe I fay can gaine, and the Saylers liue going for fhares, leffe then the third part of their labours, and yet fpend as much time in going and comming, as in ftaying there, fo fhort is the feafon of fifhing; why fhould wee more doubt, then *Holland*, *Portugale*, *Spaniard*, *French*, or other, but to doe much better then they, where there is victuall to feede vs, wood of all forts, to build Boats, Ships, or Barks; the fifh at our doores, pitch, tarre, mafts, yards, and moft of other neceffaries onely for making? And here are no hard Landlords to racke vs with high rents, or extorted fines to confume vs, no tedious pleas in law to confume vs with their many years difputations for Iuftice: no multitudes to occafion fuch impediments to good orders, as in popular States. So freely hath God and his Maiefty beftowed thofe bleffings on them that will attempt to obtaine them, as here euery man may be mafter and owne labour and land; or the greateft part in a fmall time. If hee haue nothing but his hands, he may fet vp this trade;

and

and by induftrie quickly grow rich; fpending but halfe that
time wel, which in *England* we abufe in idlenes, worfe or
as ill. Here is ground alfo as good as any lyeth in the
Examples of the height of forty one, forty two, forty three, &c.
altitude compar- which is as temperate and as fruitfull as any
atively. other paralell in the world. As for example, on
this fide the line Weft of it in the South Sea, is *Noua
Albion*, difcouered as is faid, by Sir *Francis Drake*. Eaft
from it, is the moft temperate part of *Portugale*, the ancient kingdomes of *Galazia, Bifkey, Nauarre, Arragon,
Catalonia, Caftilia* the olde, and the moft moderateft of
Caftilia the new, and *Valentia*, which is the greateft part
of *Spain:* which if the *Spanifh* Hiftories bee true, in the
Romanes time abounded no leffe with golde and filuer
Mines, then now the *Weft Indies;* The *Romanes* then
vfing the *Spaniards* to work in thofe Mines, as now the
Spaniard doth the *Indians.*

In *France*, the Prouinces of *Gafconic, Langadock, Auig-
non, Prouince, Dolphine, Pyamont*, and *Turyne*, are in the
fame paralell: which are the beft and richeft parts of
France. In *Italy*, the prouinces of *Genua, Lumbardy*, and
Verona, with a great part of the moft famous State of *Venice*, the Dukedoms of *Bononia, Mantua, Ferrara, Rauenna,
Bolognia, Florence, Pifa, Sienna, Vrbine, Ancona*, and the
ancient Citie and Countrey of *Rome*, with a great part of
the great Kingdome of *Naples*. In *Slauonia, Iftrya*, and
Dalmatia, with the Kingdomes of *Albania*. In *Grecia*,
                                                        that

that famous Kingdome of *Macedonia, Bulgaria, Theſſalia, Thracia,* or *Romania,* where is ſeated the moſt pleaſant and plentifull Citie in *Europe, Conſtantinople.* In *Aſia* alſo, in the ſame latitude, are the temperateſt parts of *Natolia, Armenia, Perſia,* and *China,* beſides diuers other large Countries and Kingdomes in theſe moſt milde and temperate Regions of *Aſia.* Southward, in the ſame height, is the richeſt of golde Mynes, *Chily* and *Baldiuia,* and the mouth of the great Riuer of *Plate,* &c: for all the reſt of the world in that height is yet vnknown. Beſides theſe reaſons, mine owne eyes that haue ſeene a great part of thoſe Cities and their Kingdomes, as well as it, can finde no aduantage they haue in nature, but this. They are beautified by the long labor and dilligence of induſtrious people and Art. This is onely as God made it, when he created the worlde. Therefore I conclude, if the heart and intralls of thoſe Regions were ſought: if their Land were cultured, planted and manured by men of induſtrie, iudgement, and experience ; what hope is there, or what neede they doubt, hauing thoſe aduantages of the Sea, but it might equalize any of thoſe famous Kingdomes, in all commodities, pleaſures, and conditions ? ſeeing euen the very edges doe naturally afford vs ſuch plenty, as no ſhip need returne away empty; and onely vſe but the ſeaſon of the Sea, fiſh will returne an honeſt gaine, beſide all other aduantages ; her treaſures hauing yet neuer beene opened, nor her originalls waſted, conſumed, nor abuſed.

And

The particular ftaple commodities that may be had.   And whereas it is faid, the *Hollanders* ſerue the *Eaſterlings* themſelues, and other parts that want with Herring, Ling, and wet Cod ; the *Eaſterlings*, a great part of *Europe*, with Sturgion and Cauiare ; *Cape-blanke, Spain, Portugale,* and the *Leuant,* with Mullet, and Puttargo ; *New found Land,* all *Europe,* with a thin Poore Iohn ; yet all is ſo ouerlade with fiſhers, as the fiſhing decayeth, and many are conſtrained to re turne with a ſmall fraught. *Norway,* and *Polonia,* Pitch, Tar, Maſts, and Yardes ; *Sweathland,* and *Ruſſia* Iron, and Ropes ; *France,* and *Spaine,* Canuas, Wine, Steele, Iron, and Oyle ; *Italy* and *Greece,* Silks, and Fruites. I dare boldly ſay, becauſe I haue ſeen naturally growing, or breed-ing in thoſe parts the ſame materialls that all thoſe are made of, they may as well be had here, or the moſt part of them, within the diſtance of 70 leagues for ſome few ages, as from all thoſe parts ; vſing but the ſame meanes to haue them that they doe, and with all thoſe aduantages.

The nature of ground approou-ed.   Firſt, the ground is ſo fertill, that queſtionleſs it is capable of producing any Grain, Fruits, or Seeds you will ſow or plant, growing in the Regions afore named : But it may be, not euery kinde to that perfe6tion of delicacy ; or ſome tender plants may miſ-carie, becauſe the Summer is not ſo hot, and the winter is more colde in thoſe parts wee haue yet tryed neere the Sea ſide, then we finde in the ſame height in *Europe* or *Asia ;* Yet I made a Garden vpon the top of a Rockie Ile in 43.½,

                                                            4 leagues

4 leagues from the Main, in May, that grew fo well, as it ferued vs for fallets in Iune and Iuly. All forts of cattell may here be bred and fed in the Iles, or *Peninfulaes*, fecurely for nothing. In the *Interim* till they encreafe if need be (obferuing the feafons) I durft vndertake to haue corne enough from the Saluages for 300 men, for a few trifles ; and if they fhould bee vntoward (as it is moft certaine they are) thirty or forty good men will be fufficient to bring them all in fubiection, and make this prouifion ; if they vnderftand what they doe : 200 whereof may nine monethes in the yeare be imployed in making marchandable fifh, till the reft prouide other neceffaries, fit to furnifh vs with other commodities.

In March, April, May, and halfe Iune, here is *The feafons for* Cod in abundance ; in May, Iune, Iuly, and *fifhing approoued.* Auguft Mullet and Sturgion ; whofe roes doe make Cauiare and Puttargo. Herring, if any defire them, I haue taken many out of the bellies of Cods, fome in nets ; but the Saluages compare their ftore in the Sea, to the haires of their heads : and furely there are an incredible abundance vpon this Coaft. In the end of Auguft, September, October, and Nouember, you haue Cod againe to make Cor fifh, or Poore Iohn : and each hundred is as good as two or three hundred in the *New-found Land.* So that halfe the labour in hooking, splitting, and turning, is faued : and you may haue your fifh at what Market you will, before they can haue any in *New-found Land;* where their fifh-

5 ing

ing is chiefly but in Iune and Iuly: whereas it is heere in March, April, May, September, October, and Nouember, as is faid. So that by reafon of this plantation, the Marchants may haue fraught both out and home: which yeelds an aduantage worth confideration.

Your Cor-fifh you may in like manner tranfport as you fee caufe, to ferue the Ports in *Portugale* (as *Lifbon, Auera, Porta port,* and diuers others, or what market you pleafe) before your *Ilanders* returne: They being tyed to the feafon in the open fea; you hauing a double feafon, and fifhing before your doors, may euery night fleep quietly a fhore with good cheare and what fires you will, or when you pleafe with your wiues and familie: they onely, their fhips in the maine Ocean.

The Mullets heere are in that abundance. you may take them with nets, fometimes by hundreds, where at *Cape blank* they hooke them; yet thofe but one foot and a halfe in length; thefe two, three, or foure, as oft I haue meaf-ured: much Salmon fome haue found vp the Riuers, as they haue paffed: and heer the ayre is fo temperate, as all thefe at any time may well be preferued.

Imployment for poore people and fartherleffe chil-dren. Now, young boyes and girles Saluages, or any other, be they neuer fuch idlers, may turne, carry, and return fifh, without either fhame, or any great paine: hee is very idle that is paft twelue yeares of age and cannot doe fo much: and fhe is very olde, that cannot fpin a thred to make engines to catch them.

For

For their tranfportation, the fhips that go *The facility of the plantation.* there to fifh may tranfport the firft: who for their paffage will fpare the charge of double manning their fhips, which they muft doe in *New-found Land*, to get their fraught; but one third part of that companie are onely but proper to ferue a ftage, carry a barrow, and turne Poor Iohn: notwithftanding, they muft haue meate, drinke, clothes, and paffage, as well as the reft. Now all I defire, is but this; That thofe that voluntarily will fend fhipping, fhould make here the beft choife they can, or accept fuch as are prefented them, to ferue them at that rate: and their fhips returning leaue fuch with me, with the value of that they fhould receiue comming home, in fuch prouifions and neceffarie tooles, armes, bedding and apparell, falt, hookes, nets, lines, and fuch like as they fpare of the remainings; who till the next returne may keepe their boates and doe them many other profitable offices: prouided I haue men of ability to teach them their functions, and a company fit for Souldiers to be ready vpon an occafion; becaufe of the abufes which haue beene offered the poore Saluages, and the liberty both French or any that will, hath to deale with them as they pleafe: whofe diforders will be hard to reforme; and the longer the worfe. Now fuch order with facilitie might be taken, with euery port Towne or Citie, to obferue but this order, With free power to conuert the benefits of their fraughts to what aduantage they pleafe, and increafe their numbers as they fee occafion; who euer as
                                                        they

they are able to fubfift of themfelues, may beginne the new
Townes in *New England* in memory of their olde: which
freedome being confined but to the neceffity of the generall
good, the euent (with Gods helpe) might produce an honeft,
a noble, and a profitable emulation.

Prefent commod-   Salt vpon falt may affuredly be made; if not
ities.   at the firft in ponds, yet till they bee prouided
this may be vfed: then the Ships may tranfport Kine,
Horfe, Goates, courfe Cloath, and fuch commodities as we
want; by whofe arriuall may be made that prouifion of fifh
to fraught the Ships that they ftay not: and then if the
sailers goe for wages, it matters not. It is hard if this
returne defray not the charge: but care muft be had, they
arriue in the Spring, or elfe prouifion be made for them
againft the Winter.

Of certaine red berries called Alkermes which is worth
ten fhillings a pound, but of thefe hath been fould for thirty
or forty fhillings the pound, may yearely be gathered a good
quantitie.

Of the Mufk Rat may bee well raifed gaines, well worth
their labour, that will endeuor to make tryall of their
goodneffe.

Of Beuers, Otters, Martins, Blacke Foxes, and Furres of
price, may yearely be had 6 or 7000: and if the trade of
the *French* were preuented, many more: 25000 this yeare
were brought from thofe Northren parts into *France;* of
                                             which

which trade we may haue as good part as the *French*, if we take good courfes.

Of Mynes of Golde and Siluer, Copper, and probabili-
ties of Lead, Chriftall and Allum, I could fay much if relations were good affurances. It is true indeed, I made many
trials according to thofe inftructions I had, which doe perfwade mee I need not defpaire, but there are metalls in
the Countrey: but I am no Alchymift, nor will promife
more then I know: which is, Who will vndertake the recti-
fying of an Iron forge, if thofe that buy meate, drinke,
coals, ore, and all neceffaries at a deer rate gaine; where all
thefe things are to be had for the taking vp, in my opinion
cannot lofe.

Of woods, feeing there is fuch plenty of all forts, if thofe
that build fhips and boates, buy wood at fo great a price, as
it is in *England*, *Spaine*, *France*, *Italy*, and *Holland*, and all
other prouifions for the nourifhing of mans life; liue well
by their trade: when labour is all required to take thofe
neceffaries without any other tax; what hazard will be here,
but doe much better? And what commoditie in *Europe*
doth more decay then wood? For the goodneffe of the
ground, let vs take it fertill, or barren, or as it is: feeing it
is certaine it beares fruites, to nourifh and feed man and
beaft, as well as *England*, and the Sea thofe feuerall forts of
fifh I haue related. Thus feeing all good prouifions for
mans fuftenance, may with this facility be had, by a little
extraordinarie labour, till that tranfported be increafed; and

all

all neceffaries for fhipping, onely for labour: to which may
bee added the affiftance of the Saluages, which may eafily
be had, if they be difcreetly handled in their kindes, towards
fifhing, planting and deftroying woods. What gaines might
be raifed if this were followed (when there is but once men
to fill your ftore houfes, dwelling there, you may ferue all
Europe better and farre cheaper, then can the *Izeland* fifhers, or the *Hollanders, Cape blank,* or *New found Land:*
who muft be at as much more charge, then you) may eafily
be coniectured by his example.

An example of   2000. pound will fit out a fhip of 200. and 1
the gains vpon of a 100 tuns: If the dry fifh they both make,
euery yeare or
fix monethes re- fraught that of 200. and goe for *Spaine,* fell it
turne.   but at ten fhillings a quintall; but commonly it
giueth fifteen, or twentie; efpecially when it commeth firft,
which amounts to 3 or 4000 pound: but fay but tenne,
which is the loweft, allowing the reft for wafte, it amounts
at that rate, to 2000 pound, which is the whole charge of
your two fhips, and their equipage: Then the returne of the
money, and the fraught of the fhip for the vintage, or any
other voyage, is cleere gaine, with your fhippe of a 100
tuns of Train and oyle, befides the beuers, and other commodities; and that you may haue at home within fix
monethes, if God pleafe but to fend an ordinarie paffage.
Then fauing halfe this charge by the not ftaying of your
fhips, your victual, ouerplus of men and wages; with her
fraught thither of things neceffarie for the planters, the falt
being

being there made : as alfo may the nets and lines, within a
fhort time : if nothing were to bee expected but this, it
might in time equalize your *Hollanders* gaines, if not ex-
ceed them : they returning but wood, pitch, tarre, and fuch
groffe commodities ; you wines, oyles, fruits, filkes, and fuch
Straits commodities, as you pleafe to prouide by your Fac-
tors, againft fuch times as your fhippes arriue with them.
This would fo increafe our fhipping and failers, and fo
employ and encourage a great part of our idlers and others
that want imployments fitting their qualities at home, where
they fhame to doe that they would doe abroad ; that could
they but once tafte the fweet fruites of their owne labours,
doubtleffe many thoufands would be aduifed by good difci-
pline, to take more pleafure in honeft induftrie, then in their
humours of diffolute idleneffe.

But, to returne a little more to the particulars *A defcription of*
of this Countrey, which I intermingle thus with *the Countries in particular, and*
my proiects and reafons, not being fo fufficiently *their fituation.*
yet acquainted in thofe parts, to write fully the eftate of the
Sea, the Ayre, the Land, the Fruites, the Rocks, the People, the Gouernment, Religion, Territories, and Limita-
tions, Friends, and Foes : but, as I gathered from the
niggardly relations in a broken language to my vnder-
ftanding, during the time I ranged thofe Countries &c.
The moft Northern part I was at, was the Bay of *Pennobfcot*, which is Eaft and Weft, North and South, more
then ten leagues : but fuch were my occafions, I was con-
ftrained

ftrained to be fatiffied of them I found in the Bay, that the
Riuer ranne farre vp into the Land, and was well inhabited
with many people, but they were from their habitations,
either fifhing among the Iles, or hunting the Lakes and
Woods, for Deer and Beuers. The Bay is full of great
Ilands, of one, two, fix, eight, or ten miles in length, which
diuides it into many faire and excellent good harbours. On
the Eaft of it, are the *Tarrantines*, their mortall enemies,
where inhabit the *French*, as they report that liue with
thofe people, as one nation or family.   And Northweft of
Pennobfcot is *Mecaddacut*, at the foot of a high mountaine,
a kinde of fortreffe againft the *Tarrantines*, adioyning to
the high mountaines of *Pennobfcot*, againft whofe feet doth
beat the Sea : But ouer all the Land, Iles, or other impediments, you may well fee them fixteene or eighteene leagues
from their fituation.   *Segocket* is the next ; then *Nufconcus*,
Pemmaquid, and *Sagadahock*. Vp this Riuer where was
the Wefterne plantation are *Aumuckcawgen*, *Kinnebeck*,
and diuers others, where there is planted fome corne fields.
Along this Riuer 40 or 50 miles, I faw nothing but great
high cliffes of barren Rocks, ouergrowne with wood : but
where the Saluages dwelt there the ground is exceeding fat
and fertill. Weftward of this Riuer, is the Countrey of
Aucocifco, in the bottome of a large deepe Bay, full of
many great Iles, which diuides it into many good harbours.
Sowocotuck is the next, in the edge of a large fandy Bay,
which hath many Rocks and Iles, but few good harbours,
but

but for Barks, I yet know. But all this Coaft to *Pennobfcot*, and as farre I could fee Eaftward of it is nothing but fuch high craggy Cliffy Rocks and ftony Iles, that I wondered fuch great trees could growe upon fo hard foundations. It is a Countrie rather to affright, then delight one. And how to defcribe a more plaine fpectacle of defolation or more barren I knowe not. Yet the Sea there is the ftrangeft fifh-pond I euer faw; and thofe barren Iles fo furnifhed with good woods, fprings, fruits, fifh, and foule, that it makes mee thinke though the Coaft be rockie, and thus affrightable; the Vallies, Plaines, and interior parts, may well (notwithftanding) be verie fertile. But there is no kingdom fo fertile hath not fome part barren : and *New England* is great enough, to make many Kingdomes and Countries, were it all inhabited. As you paffe the Coaft ftill Weftward, *Accominticus* and *Paffataquack* are two con-uenient harbors for fmall barks; and a good Countrie, within their craggie cliffs. *Angoam* is the next; This place might content a right curious iudgement : but there are many fands at the entrance of the harbor: and the worft is, it is inbayed too farre from the deepe Sea. Heere are many rifing hilles, and on their tops and defcents many corne fields, and delightfull groues. On the Eaft, is an Ile of two or three leagues in length; the one halfe, plaine morifh graffe fit for pafture, with many faire high groues of mulberrie trees gardens: and there is alfo Okes, Pines, and

7   other

other woods to make this place an excellent habitation, beeing a good and fafe harbor.

Naimkeck though it be more rockie ground (for *Angoam* is fandie) not much inferior; neither for the harbor, nor any thing I could perceiue, but the multitude of people. From hence doth ftretch into the Sea the faire headland *Tragabigzanda,* fronted with three Iles called the three *Turks heads :* to the North of this, doth enter a great Bay, where wee founde fome habitations and corne fields : they report a great Riuer, and at leaft thirtie habitations, doo poffeffe this Countrie. But becaufe the *French* had got their Trade, I had no leafure to difcouer it. The Iles of *Mattahunts* are on the Weft fide of this Bay, where are many Iles, and queftionleffe good harbors : and then the Countrie of the *Maffachufets,* which is the Paradife of all thofe parts: for, heere are many Iles all planted with corne; groues, mulberries, faluage gardens, and good harbors : the Coaft is for the moft part, high clayie fandie cliffs. The Sea Coaft as you paffe, fhewes you all along large corne fields, and great troupes of well proportioned people : but the *French* hauing remained heere neere fixe weckes, left nothing for vs to take occafion to examine the inhabitants relations, *viz.* if there be neer three thoufand people vpon thefe Iles; and that the Riuer doth pearce many daies iourneies the intralles of that Countrey. We found the people in thofe parts verie kinde; but in their furie no leffe valiant. For, vpon a quarrell wee had with one of them,

hee

hee onely with three others croffed the harbor of *Quona-haffit* to certaine rocks whereby wee muft paffe ; and there let flie their arrowes for our fhot, till we were out of danger.

Then come you to *Accomack*, an excellent good harbor, good land ; and no want of any thing, but induftrious people. After much kindneffe, vpon a fmall occafion, wee fought alfo with fortie or fiftie of thofe : though fome were hurt, and fome flaine ; yet within an houre after they became friendes. *Cape Cod* is the next prefents it felfe : which is onely a headland of high hils of fand, ouergrowne with fhrubbie pines, hurts, and fuch trafh ; but an excellent harbor for all weathers. This *Cape* is made by the maine Sea on the one fide, and a great Bay on the other in forme of a fickle : on it doth inhabit the people of *Pawmet :* and in the bottome of the Bay, the people of *Chawum*. Towards the South and South weft of this *Cape*, is found a long and dangerous fhoale of fands and rocks. But fo farre as I incircled it, I found thirtie fadom water aboard the fhore and a ftrong current : which makes mee thinke there is a Channell about this fhoale ; where is the beft and great-eft fifh to be had, Winter and Summer, in all that Countrie. But, the Saiuages fay there is no Channell, but that the fhoales beginne from the maine at *Pawmet*, to the Ile of *Nausit ;* and fo extends beyond their knowledge into the Sea. The next to this is *Capawack*, and thofe abounding Countries of copper, corne, people, and mineralls ; which I

went

went to difcouer this laft yeare: but becaufe I mifcarried
by the way, I will leaue them, till God pleafe I haue better
acquaintance with them.

A good Countrie.

The *Maffachufets*, they report, fometimes haue
warres with the *Bafhabes* of *Pennobfkot;* and are
not alwaies friends with them of *Chawum* and their alliants:
but now they are all friends, and haue each trade with other,
fo farre as they haue focietie, on each others frontiers. For
they make no fuch voiages as from *Pennobfkot* to *Cape Cod;*
feldom to *Maffachewfet*. In the North (as I haue faid) they
begunne to plant corne, whercof the South part hath fuch
plentie, as they haue what they will from them of the
North ; and in the Winter much more plenty of fifh and
foule : but both Winter and Summer hath it in the one
part or other all the yeare ; being the meane and moft
indifferent temper, betwixt heat and colde, of all the regions betwixt the Lyne and the Pole : but the furs Northward are much better, and in much more plentie, then
Southward.

The land markes.

The remarkeableft Iles and mountains for
Landmarkes are thefe ; The higheft Ile or
Sorico, in the Bay of *Pennobfkot:* but the three Iles and
a rock of *Matinnack* are much furder in the Sea ; *Metini-
cus* is alfo three plaine Iles and a rock, betwixt it and
Monahigan: Monahigan is a rounde high Ile ; and clofe
by it *Monanis,* betwixt which is a fmall harbor where we
ride. In *Damerils* Iles is fuch another: *Sagadahock* is
knowne

knowne by *Satquin*, and foure or fiue Iles in the mouth. *Smyths* Iles are a heape together, none neere them, againſt *Accominticus.* The three Turks heads are three Iles feen far to Sea-ward in regard of the headland. .

The cheefe headlands are onely *Cape Tragabigzanda* and *Cape Cod.*

The cheefe mountaines, them of *Pennobſcot :* and twink-ling mountaine of *Aucociſco ;* the greate mountaine of *Saſ-anou ;* and the high mountaine of *Maſſachuſit :* each of which you ſhall finde in the Mappe ; their places, formes, and altitude. The waters are moſt pure, proceeding from the intrals of rockie mountaines ; the hearbes and fruits are of many forts and kindes : as *Hearbs.* alkermes, currans, or a fruit like currans, mulberries, vines, reſpices, goosberries, plummes, walnuts, chefnuts, fmall nuts, &c. pumpions, gourds, ſtrawberries, beans, peaſe, and mayze : a kinde or two of flax, where with they make nets, lines and ropes both fmall and great, verie ſtrong for their quantities.

Oke, is the chiefe wood ; of which there is great difference in regard of the foyle where it *Woods.* groweth, firre, pyne, walnut, chefnut, birch, aſh, elme, cy-preſſe, ceder, mulberrie, plumtree, hazell, faxefrage, and many other forts.

Eagles, Gripes, diuerfe forts of Haukes, Cranes, Geefe, Brants, Cormorants, Ducks, Sheldrakes, *Birds.*

Teale,

Teale, Meawes, Guls, Turkies, Diue-doppers, and many
other forts, whofe names I knowe not.

Fifhes.   Whales, Grampus, Porkpifces, Turbut, Stur-
gion, Cod, Hake, Haddock, Cole, Cufk, or fmall
Ling, Shark, Mackerrell, Herring, Mullet, Bafe, Pinacks,
Cunners, Pearch, Eels, Crabs, Lobfters, Mufkles, Wilkes,
Oyfters, and diuerfe others &c.

Beafts.   Moos, a beaft bigger then a Stagge ; Deere,
red, and Fallow ; Beuers, Wolues, Foxes, both
blacke and other ; Aroughconds, Wild-cats, Beares, Otters,
Martins, Fitches, Mufquaffus, and diuerfe forts of vermine,
whofe names I know not. All thefe and diuerfe other
good things do heere, for want of vfe, ftill increafe, and
decreafe with little diminution, whereby they growe to that
abundance. You fhall fcarce finde any Baye, fhallow fhore,
or Coue of fand, where you may not take many Clampes,
or Lobfters, or both at your pleafure, and in many places
lode your boat if you pleafe ; Nor Iles where you finde not
fruits, birds, crabs, and mufkles, or all of them, for taking,
at a lowe water. And in the harbors we frequented, a little
boye might take of Cunners, and Pinacks, and fuch deli-
cate fifh, at the fhips fterne, more then fixe or tenne can
eate in a daie ; but with a cafting-net, thoufands when wee
pleafed : and fcarce any place, but Cod, Cufke, Holybut,
Mackerell, Scate, or fuch like, a man may take with a
hooke or line what he will. And, in diuerfe fandy Baies,
a man may draw with a net great ftore of Mullets, Bafes,
                                                        and

and diuerfe other forts of fuch excellent fifh, as many as
his Net can drawe on fhore : no Riuer where there is not
plentie of Sturgion, or Salmon, or both ; all which are to
be had in abundance obferuing but their feafons. But if a
man will goe at Chriftmaffe to gather Cherries in *Kent*, he
may be deceiued ; though there be plentie in Summer : fo,
heere thefe plenties haue each their feafons, as I haue ex-
preffed. We for the moft part had little but bread and
vinegar : and though the moft part of Iuly when the fifhing decaied they wrought all day, laie abroade in the Iles
all night, and liued on what they found, yet were not ficke :
But I would wifh none put himfelf long to fuch plunges ;
except neceffitie conftraine it : yet worthy is that perfon to
ftarue that heere cannot liue ; if he haue fenfe, ftrength
and health : for there is no fuch penury of thefe bleffings
in any place, but that a hundred men may, in one houre or
two, make their prouifions for a day : and hee that hath experience to manage well thefe affaires, with fortie or thirtie
honeft induftrious men, might well vndertake (if they dwell
in thefe parts) to fubiect the Saluages, and feed daily two
or three hundred men, with as good corne, fifh and flefh, as
the earth hath of thofe kindes, and yet make that labor
but their pleafure : prouided that they haue engins, that be
proper for their purpofes.

Who can defire more content, that hath fmall
meanes ; or but only his merit to aduance his
fortune, then to tread, and plant that ground

A note for men that haue great fpirits, and fmal meanes.

hee

hee hath purchafed by the hazard of his life ?   If he haue
but the tafte of virtue, and magnanimitie, what to fuch a
minde can bee more pleafant, then planting and building
a foundation for his Pofteritie, gotte from the rude earth,
by Gods bleffing and his owne induftrie, without prejudice
to any ?   If hee haue any graine of faith or zeale in Religion, what can hee doe leffe hurtfull to any ; or more agree-
able to God, then to feeke to conuert thofe poore Saluages
to know Chrift, and humanitie, whofe labors with difcretion
will triple requite thy charge and paines ?   What fo truely
futes with honour and honeftie, as the difcouering things
vnknowne ? erecting Townes, peopling Countries, inform-
ing the ignorant, reforming things vnjuft, teaching virtue ;
and gaine to our Natiue mother-countrie a kingdom to
attend her ; finde imployment for thofe that are idle, becaufe they know not what to doe : fo farre from wronging
any, as to caufe Pofteritie to remember thee ; and remem-
bring thee, euer honour that remembrance with praife ?
Confider : What were the beginnings and endings of the
Monarkies of the *Chaldeans*, the *Syrians*, the *Grecians*, and
Romanes, but this one rule ; What was it they would not doe,
for the good of the commonwealth, or their Mother-citie ?
For example : *Rome*, What made her fuch a Monarcheffe,
but onely the aduentures of her youth, not in riots at home ;
but in dangers abroade ? and the iuftice and iudgement out
of their experience, when they grewe aged.   What was
their ruine and hurt, but this ; The exceffe of idleneffe, the
                                        .   fondneffe

fondneſſe of Parents, the want of experience in Magiſtrates, the admiration of their vndeſerued honours, the contempt of true merit, their vniuſt icaloſies, their politicke incredulities, their hypocriticall feeming goodneſſe, and their deeds of ſecret lewdneſſe? finally, in fine, growing onely formall temporiſts, all that their predeceſſors got in many years, they loſt in few daies. Thoſe by their pains and vertues became Lords of the world; they by their eaſe and vices became flaues to their feruants. This is the difference betwixt the vſe of Armes in the field, and on the monuments of ſtones; the golden age and the leaden age, proſperity and miſerie, iuſtice and corruption, fubſtance and ſhadowes, words and deeds, experience and imagination, making Commonwealths and marring Commonwealths, the fruits of vertue and the concluſions of vice.

Then, who would liue at home idly (or thinke in himſelfe any worth to liue) onely to eate, drink, and ſleepe, and fo die? Or by confuming that careleſly, his friends got worthily? Or by vfing that miſerably, that maintained vertue honeſtly? Or, for being deſcended nobly, pine with the vaine vaunt of great kindred, in penurie? Or to (maintaine a filly ſhewe of brauery) toyle out thy heart, foule, and time, bafely, by ſhifts, tricks, cards, and dice? Or by relating newes of others actions, ſharke here or there for a dinner, or ſupper; deceiue thy friends, by faire promiſes, and diſſimulation, in borrowing where thou neuer intendeſt to pay; offend the lawes, furfeit with exceſſe, burden thy

7   Country,

Country, abufe thy felfe, defpaire in want, and then couzen
thy kindred, yea euen thine owne brother, and wifh thy
parents death (I will not fay damnation) to haue their
eftates? though thou feeft what honours, and rewards, the
world yet hath for them will feeke them and worthily
deferue them.

I would be fory to offend, or that any fhould miftake
my honeft meaning: for I wifh good to all, hurt to none.
But rich men for the moft part are growne to that dotage,
through their pride in their wealth, as though there were
no accident could end it, or their life. And what hellifh
care do fuch take to make it their owne miferie, and their
Countries fpoile, efpecially when there is moft neede of
their imployment? drawing by all manner of inuentions,
from the Prince and his honeft fubiects, euen the vitall
fpirits of their powers and eftates: as if their Bagges, or
Bragges, were fo powerfull a defence, the malicious could
not affault them; when they are the onely baite, to caufe
vs not to be onely affaulted; but betrayed and murdered in
our owne fecurity, ere we well perceiue it.

An example of   May not the miferable ruine of *Conftantino-*
fecure couetouf- *ple*, their impregnable walles, riches, and pleaf-
nefs.
                    .ures laft taken by the *Turke* (which are but a
bit, in comparifon of their now mightines) remember vs, of
the effects of priuate couetoufnefs? at which time the good
Emperour held himfelfe rich enough, to haue fuch rich fubiects, fo formall in all exceffe of vanity, all kinde of deli-
                                                    cacie,

cacie, and prodigalitie. His pouertie when the *Turke* be-
fieged, the citizens (whofe marchandizing thoughts were
onely to get wealth, little conceiuing the defperate refolution of a valiant expert enemy) left the Emp. fo long to his
conclufions, hauing fpent all he had to pay his young, raw,
difcontented Souldiers; that fodainly he, they, and their citie
were all a prey to the deuouring *Turke.* And what they
would not fpare for the maintenance of them who aduen-
tured their liues to defend them, did ferue onely their enemies to torment them, their friends, and countrey, and all
Chriftendome to this prefent day. Let this lamentable example remember you that are rich (feeing there are fuch
great theeues in the world to robbe you) not grudge to
lend fome proportion, to breed them that haue little, yet
willing to learne how to defend you : for, it is too late when
the deede is a-doing. The *Romanes* eftate hath beene
worfe then this : for, the meere couetoufneffe and extortion
of a few of them, fo mooued the reft, that not hauing any
imployment, but contemplation ; their great iudgements
grew to fo great malice, as themfelues were fufficient to
destroy themfelues by faction : Let this mooue you to em-
brace imployment, for thofe whofe educations, fpirits, and
iudgements, want but your purfes ; not onely to preuent
fuch accuftomed dangers, but alfo to gaine more thereby
then you haue. And you fathers that are either fo fool-
ifhly fond, or fo miferably couetous, or fo willfully ignorant,
or fo negligently careleffe, as that you will rather maintaine
your

your children in idle wantonnefs, till they growe your mafters; or become fo bafely vnkinde, as they wifh nothing
but your deaths ; fo that· both forts growe diffolute : and
although you would wifh them any where to efcape the
gallowes, and eafe your cares ; though they fpend you
here one, two, or three hundred pound a yeer ; you would
grudge to giue halfe fo much in aduenture with them, to
obtaine an eftate, which in a fmall time but with a little
affiftance of your prouidence, might bee better then your
owne.   But if an Angell fhould tell you, that any place yet
vnknowne can afford fuch fortunes ; you would not beleeue
him, no more then *Columbus* was beleeued there was any
fuch Land as is now the well knowne abounding *America ;*
much leffe fuch large Regions as are yet vnknowne, as well
in *America*, as in *Affrica*, and *Afia*, and *Terra incognita ;*
where were courfes for gentlemen (and them that would be
fo reputed) more fuiting their qualities, then begging from
their Princes generous difpofition, the labours of his fubiects, and the very marrow of his maintenance.

The Authors con-   I haue not beene fo ill bred, but I haue tafted
ditions.   of *Plenty* and *Pleafure*, as well as *Want* and
Miferic : nor doth neceffity yet, or occafion of difcontent,
force me to thefe endeauors : nor am I ignorant what fmall
thanke I fhall haue for my paines; or that many would haue
the Worlde imagine them to be of great iudgement, that
can but blemifh thefe my defignes, by their witty obiections
and detractions : yet (I hope) my reafons with my deeds,
                                                    will

will fo preuaile with fome, that I fhall not want imployment
in thefe affaires, to make the moft blinde fee his owne fenfe-
lefneffe, and incredulity; Hoping that gaine will make them
affect that, which Religion, Charity, and the Common good
cannot. It were but a poore deuice in me, To deceiue my
felfe; much more the King, and State, my Friends, and
Countrey, with thefe inducements: which, feeing his Maieftie hath giuen permiffion, I wifh all forts of worthie, honeft,
induftrious fpirits, would vnderftand: and if they defire any
further fatiffaction, I will doe my beft to giue it: Not to
perfwade them to goe onely; but goe with them: Not
leaue them there; but liue with them there. I will not
fay, but by ill prouiding and vndue managing, fuch courfes
may be taken, may make vs miferable enough: But if I
may haue the execution of what I haue proiected; if they
want to eate, let them eate or neuer digeft Me. If I performe what I fay, I defire but that reward out of the gaines
may fute my paines, quality, and condition. And if I abufe
you with my tongue, take my head for fatiffaction. If any
diflike at the yeares end, defraying their charge, by my confent they fhould freely returne. I feare not want of companie fufficient, were it but knowne what I know of thofe
Countries; and by the proofe of that wealth I hope yearely
to returne, if God pleafe to bleffe me from fuch accidents,
as are beyond my power in reafon to preuent: For, I am
not fo fimple, to thinke, that euer any other motiue then
wealth, will euer erect there a Commonweale; or draw

companie

companie from their eafe and humours at home, to ftay in
New England to effect my purpofes. And left any fhould
thinke the toile might be infupportable, though
thefe things may be had by labour, and dilligence : I affure my felfe there are who delight
extreamly in vaine pleafure, that take much more paines in
England, to enioy it, then I fhould doe heere to gaine
wealth fufficient : and yet I thinke they fhould not haue
halfe fuch fweet content : for, our pleafure here is ftill
gaines ; in *England* charges and loffe. Heer nature and
liberty affords vs that freely, which in *England* we want, or
it cofteth vs dearely. What pleafure can be more, then
(being tired with any occafion a-fhore) in planting Vines,
Fruits, or Hearbs, in contriuing their owne Grounds, to the
pleafure of their owne mindes, their Fields, Gardens, Or-
chards, Buildings, Ships, and other works, &c. to recreate
themfelues before their owne doores, in their owne boates
vpon the Sea, where man, woman and childe, with a fmall
hooke and line, by angling, may take diuerfe forts of excellent fifh, at their pleafures ?   And is it not pretty fport, to
pull vp two pence, fix pence, and twelue pence, as faft as
you can hale and veare a line ? He is a very bad fifher,
cannot kill in one day with his hooke and line, one, two,
or three hundred Cods : which dreffed and dryed, if they be
fould there for ten fhillings the hundred, though in *England* they will giue more then twentie ; may not both the
feruant, the mafter, and marchant, be well content with this
gaine ?

*The planters
pleafures, and
profits.*

gaine? If a man worke but three dayes in feauen, he may get more then hee can fpend, vnleffe he will be exceffiue. Now that Carpenter, Mafon, Gardiner, Taylor, Smith, Sailer, Forgers, or what other, may they not make this a pretty recreation though they fifh but an houre in a day, to take more then they eate in a weeke: or? if they will not eate it, becaufe there is fo much better choife; yet fell it, or change it, with the fifher men, or marchants, for any thing they want. And what fport doth yeeld a more pleafing content, and leffe hurt or charge then angling with a hooke, and croffing the fweete ayre from Ile to Ile, ouer the filent ftreames of a calme Sea? wherein the moft curious may finde pleafure, profit, and content. Thus, though all men be not fifhers: yet all men, whatfoeuer, may in other matters doe as well. For neceffity doth in thefe cafes fo rule a Commonwealth, and each in their feuerall functions, as their labours in their qualities may be as profitable, becaufe there is a neceffary mutuall vfe of all.

For Gentlemen, what exercife fhould more de- *Imployments for* light them, then ranging dayly thofe vnknowne *gentlemen.* parts, vfing fowling and fifhing, for hunting and hauking? and yet you fhall fee the wilde haukes giue you fome pleafure, in feeing them ftoope (fix or feauen after one another) an houre or two together, at the fkuls of fifh in the faire harbours, as thofe a-fhore at a foule; and neuer trouble nor torment your felues, with watching, mewing, feeding, and attending them: nor kill horfe and man with running and

crying,

crying, *See you not a hauk?*   For hunting alfo : the woods,
lakes, and riuers, affoord not onely chafe fufficient, for any
that delights in that kinde of toyle, or pleafure ; but fuch
beafts to hunt, that befides the delicacy of their bodies for
food, their fkins are fo rich, as may well recompence thy
dayly labour, with a Captains pay.

Imployments for   For labourers, if thofe that fowe hemp, rape,
labourers.   turnips, parfnips, carrats, cabidge, and fuch like;
giue 20, 30, 40, 50 fhillings yearely for an acre of ground,
and meat, drinke, and wages to vfe it, and yet grow rich ;
when better, or at leaft as good ground, may be had and
coft nothing but labour ; it feemes ftrange to me, any fuch
fhould there grow poore.

My purpose is not to perfwade children from their parents ; men from their wiues ; nor feruants from their mafters : onely, fuch as with free confent may be fpared : But
that each parifh, or village, in Citie, or Countrey, that will
but apparell their fatherleffe children, of thirteene or four-
teen years of age, or young maried people, that haue fmall
wealth to liue on ; heere by their labour may liue exceeding well : prouided alwaies that firft there bee a fufficient
power to command them, houfes to receiue them, meanes
to defend them, and meet prouifions for them ; for, any
place may bee ouerlain : and it is moft neceffarie to haue a
fortreffe (ere this grow to practice) and fufficient mafters
(as, Carpenters, Mafons, Fifhers, Fowlers, Gardiners, Hus-
bandmen, Sawyers, Smiths, Spinfters, Taylors, Weauers,

and

and fuch like) to take ten, twelue, or twentie, or as their
is occafion, for Apprentifes. The Mafters by this may
quicklie growe rich ; thefe may learne their trades themfelues, to doe the like ; to a generall and an incredible
benefit, for King, and Countrey, Mafter, and Seruant.

It would bee an hiftorie of a large volume, to *Examples of the*
recite the aduentures of the *Spanyards*, and *Por-* *Spanyard.*
tugals, their affronts, and defeats, their dangers and mife-
ries ; which with fuch incomparable honour and conftant
refolution, fo farre beyond beleefe, they haue attempted and
indured in their difcoueries and plantations, as may well
condemne vs, of too much imbecillitie, floth and negli-
gence : yet the Authors of thofe new inuentions, were held
as ridiculous, for a long time, as now are others, that doe
but feek to imitate their vnparalleled vertues. And though
we fee daily their mountaines of wealth (fprong from the
plants of their generous indeauours) yet is our fenfualitie
and vntowardneffe fuch, and fo great, that wee either igno-
rantly beleeue nothing ; or fo curioufly conteft, to preuent
wee knowe not what future euents ; that wee either fo neglect, or oppreffe and difcourage the prefent, as wee fpoile all
in the making, crop all in the blooming ; and building vpon
faire fand, rather then rough rocks, iudge that wee knowe
not, gouerne that wee haue not, feare that which is not ;
and for feare fome fhould doe too well, force fuch againft
their willes to be idle or as ill. And who is he hath iudgement, courage, and any induftrie or qualitie with vnder-

8   ftanding,

ftanding, will leaue his Countrie, his hopes at home, his
certaine eftate, his friends, pleafures, libertie, and the pre-
ferment fweete *England* doth afford to all degrees, were it
not to aduance his fortunes by inioying his deferts? whofe
profperitie once appearing, will incourage others : but it
muft be cherifhed as a childe, till it be able to goe, and
vnderftand it felfe ; and not corrected, nor oppreffed aboue
its ftrength, ere it knowe wherefore. A child can neither
performe the office, nor deedes of a man of ftrength, nor
indure that affliction He is able ; nor can an Apprentice at
the firft performe the part of a Maifter. And if twentie
yeeres bee required to make a child a man, feuen yeares
limited an apprentice for his trade : if fcarce an age be fufficient to make a wife man a States man ; and commonly, a
man dies ere he hath learned to be difcreet : If perfection
be fo hard to be obtained, as of neceffitie there muft bee
practice, as well as theorick : Let no man much condemne
this paradox opinion, to fay, that halfe feauen yeeres is
fcarce fufficient, for a good capacitie, to learne in thefe
affaires, how to carie himfelfe : and who euer fhall trie in
thefe remote places the erecting of a Colony, fhall finde at
the ende of feauen yeares occafion enough to vfe all his
difcretion : and, in the *Interim* all the content, rewards,
gaines, and hopes will be neceffarily required, to be giuen
to the beginning, till it bee able to creepe, to ftand, and
goe, yet time enough to keepe it from running, for there is
no feare it wil grow too faft, or euer to any thing ; except
libertie,

libertie, profit, honor, and profperitie there found, more binde the planters of thofe affaires, in deuotion to effect it; then bondage, violence, tyranny, ingratitude, and fuch double dealing, as bindes free men to become flaues, and honeft men turne knaues : which hath euer bin the ruine of the moft popular common-weales ; and is verie vnlikelie euer well to begin in a new.

Who feeth not what is the greateft good of *The bliffe of* the *Spanyard*, but thefe new conclufions, in *Spaine.* fearching thofe vnknowne parts of this vnknowne world ? By which meanes hee diues euen into the verie fecrets of all his Neighbours, and the moft part of the world : and when the *Portugale* and *Spanyard* had found the *Eaft* and *Weft Indies ;* how many did condemn themfelues, that did not accept of that honeft offer of Noble *Columbus ?* who, vpon our neglect, brought them to it, perfwading our felues the world had no fuch places as they had found : and yet euer fince wee finde, they ftill (from time to time) haue found new Lands, new Nations, and trades, and ftill daily dooe finde both in *Afia*, *Africa*, *Terra incognita*, and *America ;* fo that there is neither Soldier nor Mechanick, from the Lord to the begger, but thofe parts afforde them all imploiment; and difcharge their Natiue foile, of fo many thoufands of all forts, that elfe, by their floth, pride and imperfections, would long ere this haue troubled their neighbours, or haue eaten the pride of *Spaine* it felfe.

Now he knowes little, that knowes not *England* may

well

well fpare many more people then *Spaine,* and is as well
able to furnifh them with all manner of neceffaries. And
feeing, for all they haue, they ceafe not ftill to fearch for
that they hauc not, and know not; It is ftrange we fhould
be fo dull, as not maintaine that which wee haue, and pur-
fue that wee knowe.   Surely I am fure many would tafte it
ill, to bee abridged of the titles and honours of their predeceffors : when if but truely they would iudge themfelues ;
looke how inferior they are to their noble vertues, fo much
they are vnworthy of their honours and liuings : which
neuer were ordained for fhowes and fhadowes, to maintaine
idleneffe and vice ; but to make them more able to abound
in honor, by heroycall deeds of action, iudgement, pietie,
and vertue.   What was it, They would not doe both in purfe
and perfon, for the good of the Commonwealth ? which
might moue them prefently to fet out their fpare kindred in
thefe generous defignes. Religion, aboue all things, fhould
moue vs (efpecially the Clergie) if wee were religious, to
fhewe our faith by our workes ; in conuerting thofe poore
faluages, to the knowledge of God, feeing what paines the
Spanyards take to bring them to their adulterated faith.
Honor might moue the Gentrie, the valiant, and induftrious ; and the hope and affurance of wealth, all ; if wee were
that we would feeme, and be accounted.   Or be we fo far
inferior to other nations, or our fpirits fo far deiected, from
our auncient predeceffors, or our mindes fo vpon fpoile,
piracie, and fuch villany, as to ferue the *Portugall, Span-*
yard,

yard, *Dutch*, *French*, or *Turke* (as to the coft of *Europe*, too many dooe) rather then our God, our King, our Country, and our felues? excufing our idleneffe, and our bafe complaints, by want of imploiments; when heere is fuch choife of all sorts, and for all degrees, in the planting and difcouering thefe North parts of *America*.

Now to make my words more apparent by my deeds; I was the laft yeare, 1615. to haue ftaied in the Countrie, to make a more ample triall of thofe conclufions with fixteene men; whofe names were *My fecond voyage to New England.*

Thomas Dirmir.			*William Ingram.*	
Edward Stalings.			*Robert Miler.*	
Daniel Cage.	Gent.		*Dauid Cooper.*	Souldiers.
Francis Abbot.			*Iohn Patridge,*	
Iohn Gofling.			*and two boies.*	
Thomas Digbie.			*Thomas Watson*	
Daniel Baker.			*Walter Chiffick*	Sailers.
Adam Smith.			*Iohn Hall.*	

I confeffe, I could haue wifhed them as many thoufands, had all other prouifions bin in like proportion: nor would I haue had fo fewe, could I haue had meanes for more: yet (would God haue pleafed wee had fafely arriued) I neuer had the like authoritie, freedom, and prouifion, to doe fo well. The maine affiftance next God, I had to this fmall number, was my acquaintance among the Saluages; efpecially,

cially, with *Dohannida*, one of their greateft Lords; who had
liued long in *England*. By the meanes of this proud Saluage, I did not doubt but quickly to haue gotte that credit
with the reft of his friends, and alliants, to haue had as many
of them, as I defired in any defigne I intended, and that
trade alfo they had, by fuch a kind of exchange of their
Countrie commodities ; which both with eafe and fecuritie
in their feafons may be vfed. With him and diuerfe others,
I had concluded to inhabit, and defend them againft the
Terentynes ; with a better power then the *French* did them ;
whofe tyranny did inforce them to imbrace my offer, with
no fmall deuotion. And though many may thinke me more
bolde then wife, in regard of their power, dexteritie, treach-
erie, and inconftancie, hauing fo defperately affaulted and
betraied many others : I say but this (becaufe with fo many,
I haue many times done much more in *Virginia*, then I
intended heere, when I wanted that experience *Virginia*
taught me) that to mee it feemes no daunger more then
ordinarie. And though I know my felfe the meaneft of
many thoufands, whofe apprehenfiue infpection can pearce
beyond the boundes of my habilities, into the hidden things
of Nature, Art, and Reafon : yet I intreate fuch giue me
leaue to excufe my felfe of fo much imbecillitie, as to fay,
that in thefe eight yeares which I haue been conuerfant
with thefe affairs, I haue not learned there is a great difference, betwixt the directions and iudgement of experimentall
knowledge, and the fuperficiall coniecture of variable relation :

tion : wherein rumor, humor, or mifprifon haue fuch power, that oft times one is enough to beguile twentie, but twentie, not fufficient to keep one from being deceiued. Therefore I know no reason but to beleeue my own eies, before any mans imagination, that is but wrefted from the conceits of my owne proiects, and indeauours. But I honor, with all affection, the counfell and inftructions of iudiciall directions, or any other honeft aduertifement; fo farre to obferue, as they tie mee not to the crueltie of vnknowne euents.

Thefe are the inducements that thus drew me to neglect all other imployments, and fpend my time and beft abilities in thefe aduentures. Wherein, though I haue had many difcouragements by the ingratitude of fome, the malicious flanders of others, the falfeneffe of friendes, the treachery of cowards, and flowneffe of aduenturers ; but chiefly by one *Hunt*, who was Mafter of the fhip, with whom oft arguing thefe proiects, for a plantation, howeuer hee feemed well in words to like it, yet he practiced to haue robbed mee of my plots, and obferuations, and fo to leaue me alone in a defolate Ile, to the fury of famine, and all other extreamities (left I fhould haue acquainted Sir *Thomas Smith*, my Honourable good friend, and the Councell of *Virginia*) to the end, he and his affociates, might fecretly ingroffe it, ere it were knowne to the State : Yet that God that alway hath kept me from the worft of fuch practices, deliuered me from the worft of his diffimulations. Notwithftanding after

my

my departure, hee abufed the Saluages where hee came, and betrayed twenty feauen of thefe poore innocent foules, which he fould in *Spaine* for flaues, to mooue their hate againft our Nation, as well as to caufe my proceedings to be fo much the more difficult.

Now, returning in the Bark, in the fifth of Auguft, I arriued at Plimouth : where imparting thofe my purpofes to my honourable friende Sir *Ferdinando Gorge*, and fome others ; I was fo incouraged, and affured to haue the managing their authoritie in thofe parts, during my life, that I ingaged my felfe to vndertake it for them. Arriuing at London, I found alfo many promife me fuch affiftance, that I entertained *Michaell Cooper* the Mafter, who returned with mee, and others of the company. How hee dealt with others, or others with him I know not : But my publike proceeding gaue fuch incouragement, that it became fo well apprehended by fome fewe of the Southren Company, as thefe proiects were liked, and he furnifhed from London with foure fhips at Sea, before they at Plimouth had made any prouifion at all, but onely a fhip cheefely fet out by Sir *Ferdinando Gorge ;* which vpon *Hunts* late trecherie among the Saluages, returned as fhee went, and did little or nothing, but loft her time. I muft confeffe I was beholden to the fetters forth of the foure fhips that went with *Cooper ;* in that they offered mee that imploiment if I would accept it : and I finde, my refufall hath incurred fome of their difpleafures, whofe fauor and loue I exceedingly defire, if I

may

may honeftly inioy it. And though they doe cenfure me as oppofite to their proceedings ; they fhall yet ftill in all my words and deedes, finde, it is their error, not my fault, that occafions their diflike : for hauing ingaged my felfe in this bufineffe to the Weft Countrie ; I had beene verie difhoneft to haue broke my promife ; nor will I fpend more time in difcouerie, or fifhing, till I may goe with a companie for plantation : for, I know my grounds. Yet euery one that reades this booke can not put it in practice ; though it may helpe any that haue feene thofe parts. And though they endeauour to worke me euen out of my owne defignes, I will not much enuy their fortunes : but, I would bee fory their intruding ignorance fhould, by their defailements, bring thofe certainties to doubtfulneffe : So that the bufineffe profper, I haue my defire ; be it by *Londoner, Scot, Welch,* or *Englifh,* that are true fubiects to our King and Countrey : the good of my Countrey is that I feeke ; and there is more then enough for all, if they could bee content but to proceed.

At laft it pleafed Sir *Ferdinando Gorge,* and *The occafion of* Mafter Doctor *Sutliffe* Deane of *Exceter,* to con- *my returne.* ceiue fo well of thefe proiects, and my former imployments, as induced them to make a new aduenture with me in thofe parts, whither they haue fo often fent to their continuall loffe. By whofe example, many inhabitants of the weft Country, made promifes of much more then was looked for, but their priuate emulations quickly qualified that heat in

9 the

the greater number ; fo that the burden lay principally on them, and fome few Gentlemen my friends, in *London*. In the end I was furnifhed with a fhip of 200. and another of 50. But ere I had fayled 120 leagues, fhee broke all her mafts ; pumping each watch 5 or 6000 ftrokes : onely her fpret faile remayned to fpoon before the wind, till we had

My reimbark- reaccommodated a Iury maft, and the reft, to re-
ment, incounters turne for *Plimouth*. My Vice-Admirall beeing
with pyrats and
imprifonment by loft, not knowing of this, proceeded her voyage :
the French. Now with the remainder of thofe prouifions, I got out again in a fmall Barke of 60 tuns with 30 men (for this of 200 and prouifion for 70) which were the 16 before named, and 14 other faylors for the fhip. With thofe I fet faile againe the 24 of Iune : where what befell me (becaufe my *actions* and *writings* are fo publicke to the world, enuy ftill feeking to fcandalize my endeauours, and feeing no power but death, can ftop the chat of ill tongues, nor imagination of mens mindes) left my owne relations of thofe hard euents, might by fome conftructors, be made doubtfull, I haue thought it beft to infert the examinations of thofe proceedings, taken by Sir *Lewis Stukley* a worthie Knight, and Vice admirall of *Deuonfhire ;* which were as followeth.   *The*

The examination of Daniel Baker, *late Steward to Captaine*
Iohn Smith *in the returne of* Plimouth ; *taken before Sir*
Lewis Stukley *Knight, the eight of December* 1615.

Who faith, being chafed two dayes by one *Captaine Fry his ship* 140 *tuns,* 36 *caſt peeces and murderers,* 80 *men ; of which* 40, *or* 50, *were maſter gunners.*
Fry, an Englifh Pirate, that could not board vs,
by reafon of foule weather, *Edmund Chambers,*
the Mafter, *Iohn Minter,* his mate, *Thomas Digby*
the Pilot, and others importuned his faide Captaine to yeeld; houlding it vnpoffible hee fhould defend himfelfe : and that the faide Captaine fhould fend them his
boate, in that they had none : which at laft he concluded
vpon thefe conditions, That *Fry* the Pyrate fhould vow not
to take any thing from Captaine *Smith,* that might ouer-
throwe his voyage, nor fend more Pirates into his fhip then
hee liked off; otherwaies, he would make fure of them he
had, and defend himfelfe againft the reft as hee could.

More : he confeffeth that the quarter-mafters and *Cham-*
bers receiued golde of thofe Pirats ; but how much, he
knoweth not : Nor would his Captain come out of his
Caben to entertaine them ; although a great many of them
had beene his faylers, and for his loue would haue wafted
vs to the Iles of *Flowers.*

At *Fyall,* wee were chafed by two French *The one of* 200, *the other* 20.
Pyrats, who commanded vs Amaine. *Chambers,*
Minter, Digby, and others, importuned againe the Captaine
to yeeld; alledging they were *Turks,* and would make them
all

all flaues: or *Frenchmen*, and would throw them all ouer
board if they fhot but a peece ; and that they were entertained to fifh, and not to fight: vntill the Captaine vowed
to fire the powder and fplit the fhip, if they would not
ftand to their defence ; whereby at laft we went cleere of
them, for all their fhot.

The Admirall 140   At *Flowers* wee were chafed by foure French
tuns, 12 peeces,
12 murderers, 90   men of warre ; all with their clofe fights afore
men, with long   and after. And this examinants Captaine hau-
piftols, pocket
piftols, musket,   ing provided for our defence, *Chambers, Minter,*
fword and po-   *Digby,* and fome others, againe importuned him
niard, the Vice-
admirall 100 tuns,   to yeeld to the fauour of thofe, againft whom
the Rere-admiral   there was nothing but ruine by fighting : But if
60, the other 80 :
all had 250 men   he would goe aboard them in that hee could
moft armed as is   fpeake *French,* by curtefie hee might goe cleere ;
faid.
fecing they offered him fuch faire quarter, and
vowed they were Proteftants, and all of *Rochell,* and had
the Kings commiffion onely to take *Spaniard, Portugales,*
and Pyrats ; which at laft hee did : but they kept this examinates Captaine and fome other of his company with
him. The next day the French men of warre went aboard
vs, and tooke what they lifted, and diuided the company
into their feuerall fhips, and manned this examinates fhip
with the Frenchmen ; and chafed with her all the fhippes
they faw : vntill about fiue or fix dayes after vpon better
confideration, they furrendered the fhip, and victualls, with
the moft part of our prouifion, but not our weapons.

More :

More : he confeſſeth that his Captain exhorted them to performe their voyage, or goe for *New found Land* to returne fraughted with fiſh, where hee would finde meanes to proceed in his plantation : but *Chambers* and *Minter* grew vpon tearms they would not ; vntill thoſe that were Souldiers concluded with their Captaines refolu- *The gentlemen* tion, they would ; feeing they had clothes, vict- *and fouldiers were euer willing* ualls, falt, nets, and lines fufficient, and expected *to fight.* their armes : and fuch other things as they wanted, the French men promiſed to reſtore, which the Captaine the next day went to feeke, and fent them about loading of commodities, as powder, match, hookes, inſtruments, his fword and dagger, bedding, aqua vitæ, his commiſſion, apparell, and many other things ; the particulars he remembreth not : But, as for the cloath, canuas, and the Captaines cloathes, *Chambers*, and his aſſociats diuided it amongſt themſelues, and to whom they beſt liked ; his Captaine not hauing any thing, to his knowledge, but his waſtecoat and breeches. And in this manner going from ſhip to ſhip, to regaine our armes, and the reſt ; they feeing a fayle, gaue chafe vntill night. The next day being very foule weather, this examinate came fo neere with the ſhip vnto the French men of warre that they fplit the maine fayle on the others fpret fayle yard. *Chambers* willed the Captaine ·come aboard, or hee would leaue him : whereupon the Captaine commanded *Chambers* to fend his boate for him. *Chambers* replyed ſhee was fplit (which was falfe) telling him hee might

might come if he would in the Admiralls boat. The Captaines anfwer was, he could not command her, nor come
when hee would : fo this examinate fell on fterne ; and that
night left his faid Captaine alone amongft the French men,
in this manner, by the command of *Chambers, Minter,* and
others.

Daniel Cage, Edward Stalings, Gentlemen ; *Walter
Chiffell, Dauid Cooper, Robert Miller,* and *Iohn Partridge,*
beeing examined, doe acknowledge and confeffe, that *Daniel Baker* his examination aboue written is true.

A double treach-   Now the caufe why the *French* detayned me
ery.   againe, was the fufpicion this *Chambers* and
Minter gaue them, that I would reuenge my felfe, vpon the
Bank, or in *New found Land,* of all the *French* I could
there incounter ; and how I would haue fired the fhip, had
they not ouerperfwaded mee : and many other fuch like
tricks to catch but opportunitie in this maner to leaue me.
And thus they returned to *Plimouth ;* and perforce with
the *French* I thus proceeded.

A fleet of nine   Being a Fleet of eight or nine fayle, we
French men of watched for the *Weft Indies* fleet, till ill weather
war, and fights
with the Span- feparated vs from the other 8. Still we fpent
iards.
     our time about the Iles neere *Fyall :* where to
keepe my perplexed thoughts from too much meditation
of my miferable eftate, I writ this difcourfe ; thinking to
haue fent it you of his Maiefties Councell, by fome fhip or
                             other :

other : for I faw their purpofe was to take all they could. At laft we were chafed by one Captain *Barra*, an *Englifh* Pyrat, in a fmall fhip, with fome twelue peeces of ordinance, about thirty men, and neer all ftarued. They fought by curtefie releefe of vs ; who gaue them fuch faire promifes, as at laft wee betrayed Captaine *Wolliflon* (his Lieftenant) and foure or fiue of their men aboard vs, and then prouided to take the reft perforce. Now my part was to be prifoner in the gun-room, and not to fpeake to any of them vpon my life : yet had *Barra* knowledge what I was. Then *Barra* perceiuing wel thefe *French* intents, made ready to fight, and *Wolliflon* as refolutely regarded not their threats, which caufed vs demurre vpon the matter longer, fom fixteene houres ; and then returned their prifoners, and fome victualls alfo, vpon a fmall compofition. The next wee tooke was a fmall *Englifh* man of *Poole* from *New found Land.* The great caben at this prefent, was my prifon ; from whence I could fee them pillage thofe poore men of all that they had, and halfe their fifh when hee was gone, they fould his poore cloathes at the maine maft, by an out-cry, which fcarce gaue each man feauen pence a peece. Not long after, wee tooke a *Scot* fraught from *Saint Michaels* to *Briftow :* hee had better fortune then the other. For, hauing but taken a boats loading of fuger, marmelade, fuckets, and fuch like, we difcried foure fayle, after whom we ftood ; who forling their maine fayles attended vs to fight. But our *French* fpirits were content onely to per-

ceiue

ceiue they were *Englifh* red croffes. Within a very fmall
time after, wee chafed foure *Spanifh* fhippes came from the
Indies: wee fought with them foure or fiue houres, tore
their fayles and fides; yet not daring to board them, loft
them. A poore Caruell of *Brafile,* was the next we chafed:
and after a fmall fight, thirteene or fourteene of her men
A prize worth being wounded, which was the better halfe, we
16000 crowns. tooke her, with 370 chefts of fugar. The next
was a *Weft Indies* man, of 160 tuns, with 1200 hides, 50
chefts of cutchanell, 14 coffers of wedgefes of filuer, 8000
A prize worth ryalls of 8, and fix coffers of the King of *Spaines*
200000 crownes. treafure, befides the pillage and rich coffers of
many rich paffengers. Two monethes they kept me in this
manner to manage their fights againft the *Spaniards,* and
be a prifoner when they tooke any *Englifh.* Now though
the Captaine had oft broke his promife, which was to put
me a-fhore on the Iles, or the next fhip he tooke; yet, at
laft, he was intreated I fhould goe for *France* in the Caruell
of fugar: himfelf refolued ftill to keepe the Seas. Within
two dayes after, we were haled by two *Weft Indy* men: but
when they faw vs waue them for the King of *France,* they
gaue vs their broad sides, fhot through our mayne maft and
fo left vs. Hauing liued thus, neer three moneths among
those French men of warre; with much adoe, we arriued at
the *Gulion,* not far from *Rochel;* where inftead of the great
promifes they alwaies fed me with, of double fatiffaction,
and full content, they kept me fiue or fix daies prifoner in
the

the Caruell, accufing me to bee him that burnt their Colony in *New France;* to force mee giue them a difcharge before the Iudge of the Admiralty, and fo ftand to their curtifie for fatiffaction, or lie in prifon, or a worfe mifchiefe. To preuent this choife, in the end of fuch a ftorme that beat them all vnder Hatches, I watched my op- *My efcape from* portunity to get a-fhore in their boat; where- *the French men.* into, in the darke night, I fecretly got: and with a halfe · pike that lay by me, put a drift for *Rat Ile:* but the Current was fo ftrong and the Sea fo great, I went a drift to Sea; till it pleafed God the winde fo turned with the tide, that although I was all this fearfull night of gufts and raine, in the Sea, the fpace of 12 houres, when many fhips were driuen a fhore, and diuerfe split (and being with fculling and bayling the water tired, I expected each minute would . sinke mee) at laft I arriued in an oazie Ile by *Charowne;* were certaine fowlers found mee neere drowned, and halfe dead, with water, colde, and hunger. By those, I found meanes to gette to *Rochell;* where I vnderftood the man of warre which we left at Sea, and the rich prize was fplit, the Captaine drowned and halfe his companie the fame night, within feauen leagues of that place, from whence I efcaped alone, in the little boate, by the mercy of God; far beyond all mens reafon, or my expectation. Arriuing at *Rochell,* vpon my complaint to the Iudge of the Admiralitie, I founde many good words, and faire promifes; and ere long many of them that efcaped drowning, tolde mee the newes they

heard

heard of my owne death: thefe I arrefting, their feuerall examinations did fo confirme my complaint, it was held proofe fufficient.   All which being performed according to

Sir Thomas Ed- the order of iuftice, from vnder the iudges hand;
munds.   I prefented it to the Englifh Ambaffador then at *Burdeaux*, where it was my chance to fee the arriuall of the Kings great mariage brought from *Spaine*.   Of the wrack of the rich prize fome 36000. crownes worth of goods came

They betraied a fhore and was faued with the Caruell, which I
mee hauing the did my beft to arreft : the Iudge did promife me
broad fcale of
England : and I fhould haue iuftice ; what will bee the conclu-
neere twentie
fayle of Englifh fion as yet, I know not.   But vnder the colour
more, befides to take Pirats and Weft-Indie men (becaufe the
them concealed
in like maner *Spanyards* will not fuffer the *French* trade in
were betrayed the Weft-Indies) any goods from thence, though
that year.
they take them vpon the Coaft of *Spaine*, are . lawfull prize ; or from any of his territories out of the limits of *Europe*.

My returne for   Leauing thus my bufineffe in *France*, I re-
England, 1615. turned to Plimouth, to find them that had thus buried me amongft the *French :* and not onely buried mee, but with fo much infamy, as fuch trecherous cowards could fuggeft to excufe their villanies : But my clothes, bookes, inftruments, Armes, and what I had, they fhared amongft them, and what they liked ; fayning, the *French* had all was wanting ; and had throwne them into the Sea, taken their fhip, and all, had they not runne away and left me as they did.

did. The cheeftaines of this mutinie that I could finde, I laied by the heeles; the reft, like themfelues, confeffed the truth as you haue heard. Now how I haue or could pre-uent thefe accidents, I reft at your cenfures. But to the matter.

Newfound-land at the firft, I haue heard, was held as def-perate a fifhing, as this I proiect in *New England. Placen-tia,* and the *Banke,* were alfo as doubtfull to the *French:* But, for all the difafters happened mee, the bufineffe is the fame it was: and the fiue fhips (whereof one was reported more then three hundred tunnes) went forward; and found fifh fo much, that neither Izeland-man, nor Newfound-land-man, I could heare of hath beene there, will goe any more to either place, if they may goe thither. So, that vpon the returne of my Vice-admirall that proceeded on her voyage when I fpent my mafts, from Pli-mouth this yeare are gone foure or fiue faile: and from London as many; onely to make voyages of profit: where the Englifhmen haue

The fuceffe of my vice Admi-rall: and the foure fhips of London, from New England.

yet beene, all their returnes together (except Sir *Fr. Popp-hames*) would fcarce make one a fauer of neere a douzen I could nominate; though there be fifh fufficient, as I per-fwàde my felfe, to fraught yearely foure or fiue hundred fayle, or as many as will goe. For, this fifhing ftretcheth along the Coaft from *Cape Cod* to *Newfound-land,* which is feauen or eight hundered miles at the leaft; and hath his courfe in the deepes, and by the fhore, all the yeare long;
keeping

keeping their hants and feedings as the beafts of the field, and the birds of the aire. But, all men are not fuch as they fhould bee, haue vndertaken thofe voiages: and a man that hath but heard of an inftrument, can hardly vfe it fo well, as hee that by vfe hath contriued to make it. All the *Romanes* were not *Scipioes:* nor all the *Geneweles, Colum-bufes:* nor all *Spanyards, Cortefes:* had they diued no deeper in the fecrets of their difcoueries, then wee, or ftopped at fuch doubts and poore accidentall chances; they had neuer beene remembred as they are: yet had they no fuch certainties to begin as wee. But, to conclude, *Adam* and *Eue* did firft beginne this innocent worke, To plant the earth to remaine to pofteritie ; but not without labour, trouble and induftrie. *Noe*, and his family, beganne againe the fecond plantation ; and their feede as it ftill increafed, hath ftill planted new Countries, and one countrie another : and fo the world to that eftate it is. But not without much hazard, trauell, difcontents, and many difafters. Had thofe worthie Fathers and their memorable off-fpring not beene more dilligent for vs now in thefe Ages, then wee are to plant that yet vnplanted, for the after liuers : Had the feede of *Abraham*, our Sauiour Chrift, and his Apoftles, expofed themfelues to no more dangers to teach the Gof-pell, and the will of God then wee ; Euen wee our felues, had at this prefent been as Saluage, and as miferable as the moft barbarous Saluage yet vnciuilized. The *Hebrewes*, and *Lacedæmonians*, the *Goths*, the *Grecians*, the *Romanes*,

and

and the reſt, what was it they would not vndertake to
inlarge their Territories, enrich their ſubiects, reſiſt their
enemies? Thoſe that were the founders of thoſe great
Monarchies and their vertues, were no ſiluered idle golden
Phariſes, but induſtrious iron-ſteeled *Publicans*: They regarded more prouiſions, and neceſſaries for their people,
then iewels, riches, eaſe, or delight for themſelues. Riches
were their ſeruants, not their Maiſters. They ruled (as
Fathers, not as Tyrantes) their people as children, not as
ſlaues: there was no diſaſter, could diſcourage them; and
let none thinke they incountered not with all manner of
incumbrances. And what haue euer beene the workes of
the greateſt Princes of the earth, but planting of countries,
and ciuilizing barbarous and inhumane Nations, to ciuilitie
and humanitie? whoſe eternall actions, fill our hiſtories.
Lastly, the *Portugales*, and *Spanyards:* whoſe euerliuing
actions, before our eyes will teſtifie with them our idle-
neſſe, and ingratitude to all poſterities, and the neglect of
our duties in our pietie and religion we owe our God, our
King, and Countrie; and want of charity to thoſe poore
ſaluages, whoſe Countrie wee challenge, vſe and poſſeſſe;
except wee bee but made to vſe, and marre what our Fore-
fathers made, or but onely tell what they did, or eſteeme
our ſelues too good to take the like paines. Was it vertue
in them, to prouide that doth maintaine vs? and baſeneſs
for vs to doe the like for others? Surely no. Then ſeeing
we are not borne for our ſelues, but each to helpe other and
our

our abilities are much alike at the houre of our birth and
the minute of our death: Seeing our good deedes, or our
badde, by faith in Chrifts merits, is all we haue to carrie
our foules to heauen, or hell: Seeing honour is our liues
ambition; and our ambition after death, to haue
an honourable memorie of our life : and
feeing by noe meanes wee would bee
abated of the dignities and glories
of our Predeceffors ; let vs
imitate their vertues to
bee worthily their
fucceffors.

F I N I S.

At London *printed the* 18. *of Iune in
the yeare of our* Lord 1616.

To his worthy Captaine,
the Author.

OFt thou haſt led, when I brought vp the Rere
*   In bloodie wars, where thouſands haue bin ſlaine.*
Then giue mee leaue, in this ſome part to beare ;
And as thy ſeruant, heere to read my name.
*   Tis true, long time thou haſt my Captaine beene*
In the fierce wars of Tranſiluania :
*   Long ere that thou* America *hadſt ſeene,*
Or led waſt captiued in Virginia ;
*   Thou that to paſſe the worlds foure parts doſt deeme*
No more, then t'were to goe to bed, or drinke,
*   And all thou yet haſt done, thou doſt eſteeme*
As nothing ; This doth cauſe mee thinke
*   That thou I'aue ſeene ſo oft approu'd in dangers*
(And thrice captiu'd, thy valor ſtill hath freed)
*   Art yet preſerued, to connert theſe ſtrangers :*
By God thy guide, I truſt it is decreed.
*   For mee : I not commend, but much admire*
Thy England yet vnknowne to paſſers by-her.
*   For it will praiſe it ſelfe in ſpight of me ;*
Thou, it, it thou, to all poſteritie.

Your true friend,

and fouldier,

Ed. Robiſon.

To my honeſt Captaine,
the Author.

M<small>*Alignant Times ! What can be ſaid or don,*</small>
   But ſhall be cenſur'd and traduc't by ſome !
This worthy Work, which thou haſt bought ſo dear,
Ne thou, nor it, Detractors neede to fear.
Thy words by deedes ſo long thou haſt approu'd,
Of thouſands knowe thee not thou art belou'd.
   And this great Plot will make thee ten times more
   Knowne and belou'd, than ere thou wert before.
I neuer knew a Warryer yet, but thee,
From wine, Tobacco, debts, dice, oaths, ſo free.
   I call thee Warrier : *and I make the bolder ;*
   For, many a Captaine *now, was neuer Souldier.*
Some ſuch may ſwell at this : but (to their praiſe)
When they haue don like thee, my Muſe ſhall raiſe
   Their due deſerts to Worthies yet to come,
   To liue like thine (admir'd) till day of Doome.

Your true friend,

      ſometimes your ſoldier,

        T<small>HO.</small> C<small>ARLTON.</small>

INDEX.

INDEX.